TRADITIONAL ENGLISH COOKING

Cookery advisor: Jane Grigson

Line illustrations by Prue Theobalds

TRADITIONAL ENGLISH COOKING

A book of country recipes

Kathie Webber

B. T. BATSFORD LTD, LONDON

ISBN 0 7134 3887 8

Phototypeset in Linotron 202 Aster by
Western Printing Services Ltd, Bristol
and printed in Great Britain by
Robert MacLehose Ltd
Glasgow Scotland
for the publishers
B. T. Batsford Ltd
4 Fitzhardinge Street
London W1H 0AH

Contents

Introduction

It is impossible to unravel all but a few threads of the history of English cookery and there are many different dishes, considered traditional, which were in fact influenced by the French and Italians from the fifteenth century, and earlier by the Romans, who, for example, are reputed to have brought cherries to England. But at what point in our history does one draw a dividing line, deciding that all ideas prior to a certain date must by now be considered absorbed and therefore thoroughly English? Certainly English cookery would be less interesting if we ignored tomatoes, potatoes, globe artichokes, the cauliflower and the turkey.

English food was not greatly influenced by court cookery, or by the more elegant ideas of imported chefs. It owed more to the manor house and large country home style of cooking and so remained rustic. There were no sweeping changes until the industrial revolution of the nineteenth century which brought us machinery, factories and a very different kind of poverty, workers existing largely on tea, bread and potatoes without even the occasional egg or vegetable available to the poor of the countryside.

A greater understanding of science led us to canning and food regulations in order to prevent adulteration of foods with harmful ingredients, but it also led to the refining of flours for 'white' bread. The railways brought more fresh produce to the towns and in better condition than before, but where was the gain when prior to the spread of brick-built factories, the land was used for market gardening? More commercially prepared foods could be bought as we learned the advantages of chilling and packaging but fewer were home-cooked. Obviously, we have never felt as strongly about food as have the French, otherwise we would never have allowed the deterioration of so much of our produce and the greater percentage of manufactured foods in our kitchens.

There is a tremendous revival at present of everything old. Restaurants, good and indifferent alike, serve newly discovered old dishes, which are often wonderful additions to our culinary repertoire.

So, too, there is a revival of kitchen gardening, sponsored commercially by the seedsmen, for that is their job, but taken up in small ways by people who discover the joy of planting seeds, watching them grow, then bringing the produce, however small or mis-shapen, into the kitchen for applause. Economically, we are ripe for a revival of growing our own fruit and vegetables, although I do not think that many of us will return to the older ways of keeping a cow, a pig, a few chickens and a duck or two; they demand more time than the average person with a job away from home can manage.

Cookbooks continue to be published, although I think there are too many which give recipes combining toast, sardines, cheese slices and bought pickle. But to redress the balance, there are enough facsimiles of old books being printed and so Eliza Acton, Maria Rundell, Elizabeth Raffald and Hannah Glasse can be read and enjoyed by everyone. Mrs Beeton has long been available, not only in the original which was printed in many different editions so that one can always find a copy at a reasonable price, but in new editions, updated for today's world. There are many good recipes in the collection submitted to the magazine she edited with her husband which were printed eventually in the great book.

Time, as always, is the devil of good food. Boiled cabbage takes little time; dressing it with butter, caraway seeds, or perhaps cooking a little onion with the cabbage, takes a while longer and because of the pressure of our lives, we opt for the quickest, which is rarely the best.

For this book on English rural food, I have chosen recipes which I particularly like, ignoring the barons of beef and crown roasts of lamb, opting, instead, for Welsh rabbit, chicken and parsley pie, creamed parsnips, elderberry and apple jam, to show how good our rural and traditional food can be, and how inexpensive it can be.

I have borrowed recipes from the great women writers of yesterday, and of today, notably Jane Grigson. It is interesting to note that in England the tradition of women writers continues. Mrs Glasse and Mrs Raffald dominated the eighteenth century just as Mrs Rundell, Eliza Acton and Mrs Beeton did the nineteenth century. Today, Michael Smith and Robert Carrier are still the exceptions, both producing recipes in the grander style. Essentially, we are a nation of domestic cooks. Foods are preferred simply cooked, we are suspicious of over-decorated dishes, or those covered with sauces. We like to see what we are eating and our palates are not trained in the appreciation of many flavours in any one dish.

The fact that we have now accepted pasta, Chinese foods and a growing number of new vegetables and fruits, is a measure of our new attitudes in cookery. I hope this growing awareness will flourish for then quality will not be left a poor second to convenience.

Note
The measurements used in this book are imperial, metric and American in that order. It is advisable to use only one set and not to mix them, since they are not always exact conversions.

Dairy Produce

Sometimes I try to imagine the discovery of the products which can be made from milk: butter, cheese, yoghurt and cream. Cream does not overwork my imagination because it floats and would have been skimmed off the milk, but to turn it into butter, to make cheeses out of it, and to discover that the stomach lining of the cow produces rennet which lightly sets milk—that must have been very exciting. But perhaps they were greeted as disasters, the fresh milk useless, as when badly kept, wet grain fermented to form an alcoholic liquid.

Butter is one of the best cooking media; it is also a light preservative, used to pot shrimps and meat and to seal mousses of fish. You should try making some at home, in addition to yoghurt and clotted cream, all of which can be made without specialized equipment.

Our tradition of making soft cream cheeses such as the Brie and Camembert, those masterpieces of the French dairy, has languished but we do have a good variety of hard cheeses: Cheddar, Cheshire, Gloucester, Wensleydale, Lancashire, Stilton, Caerphilly etc., all with different characteristics. Cheddar is the most useful all-purpose cheese; Lancashire is the best for toasted cheese and for Welsh rabbit, but where now can one get the cheese which crumbles as it is cut? Like the rest, Lancashire has been reduced to a rubbery consistency.

There are a growing number of shops which take the trouble to sell good cheese. When in London, pay a visit to Paxton and Whitfield in Jermyn Street which runs parallel with Piccadilly to the south. There they understand cheese, provide small pieces for sampling and sell only the best. There you will appreciate the individuality of each cheese variety. You will also pay more for the matured cheese which is the one to use for cooking. Paradoxically, we buy the cheapest, thinking that it will not matter for cooking. It does.

Making yoghurt

Too many fancy machines requiring electricity are sold for making yoghurt, turning a simple process into something complicated and time-consuming. Always the best results come from a bowl, cloth cover and an airing cupboard, or other source of gentle, constant warmth.

1 pt (600 ml/2½ cups) milk
1 level tbsp (15 ml/1 good tbsp) dried skimmed milk powder
1 level tbsp (15 ml/1 good tbsp) natural yoghurt

Untreated milk is the best for yoghurt, but you can use pasteurized, homogenized, sterilized or ultra-heat-treated milk, although these two latter milks will give a thinner yoghurt. Dried skimmed milk powder gives a thicker, creamier yoghurt, and as a starting culture, use bought yoghurt from a carton. Thereafter, you should save some of your own to begin the next day's batch.

Heat the milk to boiling point then allow it to cool to 120°F (49°C). Stir in the dried milk powder and whisk in the yoghurt. Leave the mixture in a bowl or pour it into clean, warm jars or cartons, covering the yoghurt container(s) with two towels. The next step is to keep the yoghurt in a constant temperature of not less than 100°F (38°C) for 4 to 6 hours. I find the airing cupboard successful; a friend with an Aga cooker leaves her yoghurt in the coolest oven, and another yoghurt-maker I know uses a polystyrene box. Unfortunately, there are no hard and fast rules for this step because it requires experiment. Your household might have too hot an airing cupboard, but a thick cloth on top of the boiler may produce the right temperature. The longer the yoghurt is left the thicker it will be, although after it is set, the acid flavour becomes stronger the longer it is left working in the warmth. When the yoghurt is set, you can transfer it to the refrigerator to chill. Save a tablespoon of your own yoghurt to make the next batch, spooning it from the centre of the yoghurt. After 3 or 4 batches, it is advisable to begin again with commercially prepared yoghurt, choosing one with no additives as your starter.

Clotted cream

Although it is possible to buy clotted cream throughout the country, it never has quite the fresh and delicious flavour of the cream served with scones and jam in Devon and Cornwall. Even the tins prepared specially to be posted home are disappointing and rarely stand up to a train or car ride out of their home counties, let alone the vagaries of the postal system. It is perfectly possible to make clotted cream with rich Channel Islands or gold top milk using the domestic cooker and scalding it slowly, the slower the better.

Pour 3 pt (1½ l/7 cups) gold top milk into a large saucepan and leave it in the refrigerator for at least 12 hours for the cream to rise. Although this is the maximum time you can leave the milk in summer, in winter it may be left safely for up to 24 hours. Carefully transfer the pan to the stove and heat it as gently as possible until the cream produces a raised ring around the edge. This will take 1 hour 15 minutes, the time depending very much on the size of the pan, the thickness of it and the heat underneath it. Never let the milk boil, because this produces a thick skin on the cream. When it has scalded sufficiently, the cream on top will look thick and wrinkled. Often the surface is covered with smaller rings. Again, steadily transfer the pan to the refrigerator. It is most important that the surface of the cream should remain whole when transferring the pan to and from the cooker. Next day, the thick cream can be skimmed off into a bowl, removing as thick a crust as possible at the beginning. After this layer, you may find that you can skim off another layer or so, until you reach the very thin milk underneath, which may be used for scones, but it is a poor liquid after the cream has been removed.

Butter making

The clotted cream you make turns simply into butter with some vigorous movement of a wooden spoon, and is worth trying for the taste. If you find it a pleasing occupation, produce your own butter occasionally, if only as a talking point when entertaining. The cost is competitive in monetary terms, although not in man hours. The old farmhouse where I live gained the original dairy as part of the main building at some stage in its history. This room was no specialized dairy, but a combined work room, rather like an extension of the kitchen. The cows came in to be milked, bread was baked, and clothes were washed, as the old bread oven, washing copper and fireplace which was used to heat the water testify. And to judge by the old butter paddles found, no doubt butter and cheese were made here too. Those old houses, now museums, which boast a dairy, show rooms which were kept purely for milk, butter and cheese making and were built and decorated to be kept as hygienic as possible. All-purpose dairies were probably more common than we suppose, particularly where the produce was for home and very local consumption.

Rural cheeses and cheese making

A good cheese is difficult to find nowadays and so many of us have lost the taste for the mature product with its mustardy bite and full flavour. If you regret the standardization of our cheeses, then you should subscribe to a marvellous scheme begun at the close of 1980 by Paxton and Whitfield, famous cheese purveyors situated in Jermyn Street in London. They have formed a club and each month select and mail good cheeses and interesting varieties to club members. If you wish to try Blue Vinney from Dorset, Windsor Red, Cheddar which deserves its name and the other famous British cheeses, write to them for details. Fostering the art of individual cheese making and the seasonal making of cheeses (that is making them when the milk is rich in casein and perfect for cheese making) will probably only ever be a cottage industry, never again on the scale it was when every person owning cattle made cheese. But I feel strongly that it is worth supporting. With the increasing blandness of our cheeses, Welsh rabbit, toasted cheese with ale and cheese and onion pies have lost flavour and these simple but well-balanced meals appear only as snacks today. If you have been disappointed in your cheese dishes, you should consider spending more money on mature, strong-flavoured cheese for cooking rather than buying the cheapest and most inferior quality. Enough proseletyzing. To the recipes.

Cheese and onion pie   *serves 4–6*

8 oz (225 g/2 cups) plain flour (all purpose flour)
Salt and pepper
2 level tsp (10 ml/1 scant tbsp) mustard powder
Cayenne pepper
2 oz (50 g/4 tbsp) margarine
2 oz (50 g/4 tbsp) lard
6 large onions
3 oz (75 g/6 tbsp) butter
6 oz (175 g/6 oz) good strong-flavoured cheese
Fresh parsley or thyme

Sift the flour, a good pinch of salt, mustard and a little cayenne pepper into a bowl. Cut in the margarine and lard and rub in the fats until the mixture looks like fine breadcrumbs. Mix to a stiff dough with cold water, kneading it quickly until the pastry is smooth. Wrap it in foil or grease-proof paper and chill the pastry for 30 minutes.

Skin and roughly chop the onions. Heat the butter in a large frying pan and fry the onions gently for 10 to 15 minutes, stirring them occasionally, until they are a rich golden brown. Remove from the heat and season them with salt and pepper. Coarsely grate the cheese, and finely chop the parsley or thyme. Two points to note here: if you can find a good Lancashire, this is the best cheese to use, but mature Cheddar, Cheshire, Leicester for its colour or Gloucester are all an improvement on the rubbery vacuum-packed blocks. Secondly, fresh herbs are essential, dried ones will not do. In winter, when fresh herbs are scarce, use what you have. Perennial sage (in small quantities) is wonderful in this pie but do add some parsley which you can buy all year round.

Roll the pastry on a lightly floured board and use half of it to line a fairly deep pie dish. Layer the onions and butter, cheese and herbs in the dish, filling it completely. Moisten the pastry edge and cover the pie, pressing the edges gently to seal them. Trim and decorate them. Brush the pastry with a little beaten egg, or egg mixed with a little water or with milk and bake it in a hot oven at 400°F (200°C), gas mark 6 for 25 to 30 minutes or until the crust is golden brown and cooked.

This is a rich, tasty and cheap but satisfying supper dish. A version for eating cold, which will hold its shape when cut, can be made by adding some very fine breadcrumbs to the layers. About 2 oz (50 g/¾ cup) is the correct quantity, and wholemeal breadcrumbs are better than white ones.

Curd cheese

Before refrigerators were a standard piece of equipment in every kitchen and dairy, milk soured, and although the greyish curds and whey in the bottle were greeted with a brisk little noise of annoyance, the frugal housewife at once considered making scones, or turning the soured milk into a curd cheese. My mother prepared it simply, pouring the curds and whey into a piece of muslin lining a sieve, tying the muslin into a bag and hanging it on the taps of the kitchen sink so that it could drip during the day. Towards evening, when the bag was dry, the solid curd cheese was turned on to a plate, seasoned and mixed with a little salt and sent to table with bread and butter for tea. I was always pleading with my mother to allow some milk to sour so we could have curd cheese. I do try the same method today, but am never quite as successful, part of the reason being the lack of the old stone sink which kept the swinging bag cool even in the hottest weather. Nowadays, unless the sieve is put over a basin and the whole lot put in the fridge, you achieve a rather unpleasant off-tasting white paste. But with care, a fresh-tasting cheese can be the result. If you leave the curd cheese sweet, use it to make Yorkshire curd tarts, the forerunner of the splendid cheesecakes which American Jewish cookery has raised to perfection.

Yorkshire curd tarts *makes 15*

7 oz (198 g/7 oz packet) puff pastry
6 oz (175 g/6 oz) fresh curd cheese
1½ oz (40 g/3 tbsp) unsalted butter
1 egg, size 3 or 4
½ lemon
1½ oz (40 g/3 tbsp) castor sugar
1½ oz (40 g/4½ tbsp) sultanas
Ground cinnamon
1 tbsp (15 ml/1 good tbsp) double cream (heavy cream)

Allow the pastry to thaw completely then roll it on a lightly floured board, cut it into rounds with a fluted cutter and use these rounds to line patty or tart tins.

Mix the curd cheese and butter together and push the mixture through a nylon sieve. Separate the egg. Finely grate the rind from the lemon and stir it into the cheese with the sugar, sultanas, cinnamon, cream and egg yolk. Finally, whisk the egg white stiffly then fold it into the cheese mixture. Put a little of the curd mixture in each tin and bake the cheese tarts in a hot oven at 425°F (220°C), gas mark 7 for 15 minutes or until they are just tipped with gold and the pastry is well risen and golden brown. Serve warm, or cold, when they will lose their puffed caps, but nonetheless taste delicious.

Cheesecakes *serves 6–8*

If you look at the history of cheesecakes you will notice that rural food in this country includes many recipes for curd cheese fillings in small pastry cases. Often dried fruit or lemon rind is mixed with the cheese, sometimes a layer of jam is spread between the pastry and the filling, and occasionally you will find a larger version. But the cheesecakes which seem to be universal favourites have come to us in their present form from the United States of America where they were perfected by Jewish immigrants, particularly those from the middle European countries, Poland, Russia, Rumania and Bulgaria. Richest of all are those made with sweet cream cheese, mixed with cream and baked. Other versions are less rich, more sweet-and-sour flavoured, made from curd cheese or even cottage cheese. Less temperamental cheesecakes are made with gelatine. For a taste of Europe and traditional Jewish cookery, the following recipe is important.

1½ oz (40 g/1½ oz) plain semi-sweet biscuits
½ oz (15 g/1 tbsp) unsalted butter
4 eggs, size 2
7 oz (175 g/1 cup) castor sugar
1 lb (450 g/2 cups) soft cream cheese
2 oz (50 g/½ cup) plain flour (all purpose flour)
2 tbsp (30 ml/2–3 tbsp) lemon juice
½ pt (284 ml/1¼ cups) double cream (heavy cream)

Crush the biscuits to a fine powder with a rolling pin. Warm the butter and use it to liberally brush the base and sides of an 8 in (20 cm) loose-based cake tin. Choose a thick and fairly deep cake tin for this cheesecake. Dust the biscuit crumbs over the butter, tapping the sides of the tin to spread the crumbs in an even layer, then tip out any excess. Separate the eggs, putting the yolks in a large bowl and whisking them until they are thick, which you can do over a pan of gently simmering water using a rotary whisk, or with an electric mixer with or without the heat. Add the sugar and continue beating until the mixture is pale, thick and fluffy. It should be thick enough to hold a trail from the whisk for 5 seconds after you lift it from the mixture. Beat the cheese with a wooden spoon until it is smooth and soft then add it to the yolk mixture and continue to beat with the wooden spoon until smooth and well mixed. Beat in the flour and lemon juice. Lightly whisk the cream until it will hold a soft peak, then beat it into the cheese mixture. Lastly whisk the egg whites until they are stiff but not dry and fold them through the cheese mixture. If you find the cheese mixture is a little too stiff at first, beat a tablespoon or two of the whites into it to slacken it, then fold in the remainder. Turn the mixture into the prepared tin and cook it for 1½ hours in a slow oven at 250°F (120°C), gas mark ½ then turn off the oven and leave the cheesecake for 2 hours longer without opening the oven door. Then remove it and let it cool completely in the tin.

This is ready for dressing up. In common with all cooked cheesecakes, it will not have the completely flat smooth surface associated with gelatine-set cheesecakes and so you may prefer to cover it. This cheesecake is deep enough to cut into two layers to be sandwiched with a layer of fruit or cream.

Choose a fairly tart fruit, leaving it unsweetened. The soft fruits are perfect, and strawberries and raspberries may be left whole or mashed slightly to give a juicy purée. If you wish to use whole fruit, then make a sauce of good jam, using about 4 level tbsp (60 ml/5 level tbsp) with $\frac{1}{4}$ pt (125 ml/$\frac{2}{3}$ cup) water and 4 tsp (20 ml/1$\frac{1}{2}$ tbsp) arrowroot (cornstarch) as a thickener.

Gelatine-set cheesecake   *serves 6*

Both the cooked and the gelatine-set cheesecakes freeze well, but I think this mixture stands up better to the keeping. If you freeze either, make sure they are well thawed before serving them. Cooked cheesecakes are nicer served at room temperature whereas set cheesecakes are better when slightly chilled. Because these gelatine mixtures have a smooth finish, they require the minimum decoration. A few nuts, cream, the most perfect berries, a little grated chocolate, is all that's needed to show them off.

4 oz (100 g/4 oz) digestive biscuits (Graham crackers)
2 oz (50 g/$\frac{1}{4}$ cup) butter
1 oz (25 g/2 level tbsp) finely chopped nuts
12 oz (350 g/1$\frac{1}{2}$ cups) soft cream cheese
3 oz (75 g/$\frac{1}{4}$ cup) castor sugar
2 large lemons
$\frac{1}{2}$ oz (15 g/1 good tbsp) powdered gelatine (jello)
$\frac{1}{4}$ pt (142 ml/$\frac{2}{3}$ cup) soured cream
Sliced fresh lemon, a little cream and finely chopped, toasted nuts to
  decorate

Crush the biscuits to fairly small crumbs about the same size as the chopped nuts. Melt the butter in a pan, stir in the biscuits and nuts and mix well. Press this mixture into a well-buttered 8 in (20 cm) flan ring standing on a buttered baking sheet to make a case of an even thickness. Chill the case for 30 minutes or until it has become firm.

Beat the cheese until it is smooth, then work in the castor sugar using a wooden spoon. Finely grate the rind from the lemons and squeeze out and strain the juice. Add both to the cheese mixture. Put the gelatine with 2 tbsp (30 ml/2$\frac{1}{2}$ tbsp) cold water in a small bowl. Stand the bowl over a pan of gently simmering water and leave the gelatine to dissolve. Do not stir the gelatine, and let it dissolve slowly until the liquid becomes clear. A stir at this point will verify that all the granules have disappeared. Strain the cooled gelatine into the cheese mixture, beating well. Beat the soured cream into the cream cheese mixture and turn it at once into the biscuit case, smoothing the top lightly if necessary. Leave to set. Decorate for serving with twists of finely sliced fresh lemon, a little cream and a few finely chopped and toasted nuts.

Cottage or curd cheesecake *serves 6*

3 oz (75 g/¾ cup) self-raising flour (all purpose flour with raising agent)
Pinch of salt
4 oz (100 g/½ firmly packed cup) castor sugar
1½ oz (40 g/3 tbsp) butter
Milk
12 oz (350 g/1½ cups) cottage or curd cheese
3 large eggs, size 2 or 3
2 level tbsp (30 ml/2–3 level tbsp) arrowroot or cornflour (cornstarch)
1 level tsp (5 ml/1 good tsp) finely grated lemon rind
1 level tsp (5 ml/1 good tsp) finely grated grapefruit rind
¼ pt (142 ml/⅔ cup) double cream (heavy cream)
Fruit topping (optional)

Mix the flour with the salt and 1 oz (25 g/2 tbsp) castor sugar. Rub in the butter and mix to a dough with milk. Roll out to fit a buttered 7 in (18 cm) loose-bottomed deep cake tin. Bake the base for 20 minutes at 375°F (190°C), gas mark 5. Many recipes suggest that you sieve the cottage cheese before use but I find that this produces a rather gritty texture and prefer to blend all the ingredients in a liquidizer. If you have no liquidizer, I think the texture is better if you use the cottage cheese straight from the cartons. Separate the eggs and mix the yolks with the cottage or curd cheese, remaining sugar, the arrowroot or cornflour (cornstarch), lemon and grapefruit rinds and the cream. Mix well, either liquidizing or beating the mixture with a wooden spoon. Whisk the egg whites until they are stiff, then fold them through the cheese. Turn the mixture into the prepared cake tin and bake it in a slow oven at 300°F (150°C), gas mark 2 for 1 hour, then turn off the heat, open the oven door very slightly and leave the cheesecake for a further 30 minutes to 1 hour. Remove and cool in the tin and push up the base when completely cold. Finish if preferred with a fruit topping.

Welsh rabbit

Early cookery books give the title as 'rabbit' which then makes sense of this dish with an egg on top called buck rabbit. However, it became 'rarebit' during Victorian times, as far as I can verify. From Mrs Glasse's *The Art of Cookery Made Plain and Easy*, 1747, comes this recipe. Toast the bread on both sides, then toast the cheese on one side, lay it on the toast, and with a hot iron brown the other side. You may rub it over with mustard. She makes a distinction between Scotch rabbit and Welsh rabbit, the former recipe includes buttering the toast.

Her English rabbit recipe includes some red wine. Toast a slice of bread brown on both sides, then lay it in a plate before the fire, pour a glass of red wine over it, and let it soak the wine up; then cut some cheese very thin, and lay it very thickly over the bread, and put it in a tin oven before the fire, and it will be toasted and browned presently. Serve very hot.

Cheese and potato cakes   *makes 8*

1 lb (450 g/1 lb) freshly boiled potatoes
2 oz (50 g/¼ cup) butter
4 oz (100 g/1 cup) plain flour (all purpose flour)
4 oz (100 g/1 cup) grated hard cheese such as Cheddar or Leicester
1 egg, size 3 or 4
Salt and pepper
Good pinch of mustard powder
Dripping for frying

Drain and dry the potatoes over a gentle heat, then mash them very well. It is preferable to push the potatoes through a nylon sieve or a ricer so that there are no lumps in the mixture. Beat in the butter, flour and cheese. Beat the egg, seasoning and mustard, and work it gradually into the potatoes to make a fairly soft but not sticky dough. Knead it lightly in the bowl until it is smooth then roll it on a board using minimum flour to a

1 in (2.5 cm) thick round. Cut out smaller rounds using a 3 in (7.5 cm) plain cutter, or cut 4 in (10 cm) squares, cutting these in half diagonally. Put a little dripping on a girdle or in a heavy-based frying pan, brush it over the base when it has melted and cook the cakes a few at a time, frying them until they are golden brown on each side. These may be served buttered for tea, or with bacon and eggs for breakfast, but always freshly cooked and very hot.

Bread, butter and cheese pudding   *serves 4*

8 slices fresh white or brown bread
2 oz (50 g/¼ cup) butter
8 oz (225 g/8 oz) strong, well-flavoured cheese
½ pt (250 ml/1¼ cups) milk
2 large eggs, size 2
Salt and pepper

The crusts may be left on the bread or cut off, before spreading the slices with butter. Use a little butter to grease a shallow ovenproof dish. Coarsely grate the cheese. Press the grated cheese on to the buttered bread and cut it into triangles. Arrange the triangles in the dish, standing the bread on edge with the points sticking up, rather than laying it flat in the dish. Sprinkle with any remaining cheese that has fallen off in the arranging. Whisk the milk and eggs together, season the mixture with salt and pepper and strain it over the bread and cheese. Leave it to steep for 1 hour before baking it in a hot oven at 400°F (200°C), gas mark 6 for 20–25 minutes or until the top is crispy golden brown. Eat while piping hot.

Milk puddings   *serves 4*

I wonder when school catering will improve enough for whole generations of children to grow up without an aversion to greens, gravy or milk puddings. This hit-and-miss type of mass catering, with its attendant evils of food being kept warm, is very different from home cooking where freshly cooked milk puddings can be delicious. More variety is possible too. Enrich a pudding with a little cream, spice it, make it fruity with sultanas or top it with fruit syrups, fresh fruit or toasted nuts to provide an interesting crunchy contrast to the smoothness of the main mixture. Rice, semolina and sago all make milk puddings. Here is the basic recipe with some additions and variations.

2 oz (50 g/generous ¼ cup) whole rice, flaked rice or tapioca or
    1½ oz (40 g/¼ cup) semolina or sago
1 pt (500 ml/2½ cups) milk
1 oz (25 g/2 tbsp) granulated sugar
A piece of lemon rind   1 oz (25 g/2 tbsp) butter

Wash the whole rice well, drain it and put it into a buttered heatproof dish of approximately 1¾ pt (1 l/4½ cups) capacity. Flaked rice or tapioca will not need rinsing but can be put straight into the buttered dish. Pour in the milk and sugar and stir well, adding the lemon rind and butter, cut into small pieces. Put the pudding into the centre of a cool oven at 300°F (150°C), gas mark 2 for 2 to 2½ hours. Stir it two or three times during the first hour of cooking, to make the pudding creamy, but thereafter leave the pudding to form a lovely brown skin on top.

Semolina and sago puddings can be made quickly on top of the stove. The milk should first be heated with the lemon rind to a lukewarm temperature, then the semolina or sago sprinkled on to it, while you stir with the other hand. Cook the mixture gently, stirring all the time, until it comes to the boil and thickens. Now add the sugar and butter and cook gently for a further 5 to 8 minutes, stirring it frequently.

If you wish to bake either a semolina or sago pudding, transfer the mixture after it has thickened to a buttered ovenproof dish, sprinkling the top with nutmeg or cinnamon. Put it in a moderate oven at 350°F (180°C), gas mark 4 for 30 minutes.

Additions

Approximately 2 oz (50 g/6 tbsp) sultanas or raisins may be added to any milk pudding, with the sugar. If you wish to make a more fruit-flavoured pudding, finely grate the rind from a lemon, orange or grapefruit, adding the shreds with the sugar.

Chocolate, always a favourite, can be added too. Use about 2 oz (50 g/ 2 oz) plain cooking chocolate. Grate it and melt it with the milk as you warm it or simply stir the grated chocolate into puddings to be baked, with the sugar. A sprinkle of cinnamon will add to the flavour of the chocolate, pointing it up without imparting a strong, spicy flavour.

Syllabub   *serves 4–6*

Originally called Sille bub because it was made with a wine called Sille from the Champagne region of France, nowadays it can be a mixture of wine or some other acid such as lemon juice with milk and cream or cream alone. It was usual to put the wine or fruit juice into a bowl and milk directly into it from the cow and the rich milk, called beestings, produced by the mother after calving was particularly desirable. A note in Eliza Acton's *Modern Cookery* says, 'they are often made with equal quantities of wine and cream but are considered less wholesome without a portion of brandy'. The Victorians produced syllabubs which they called 'everlasting', potting them in pretty glasses and keeping them for three or four days to mature before setting them on the table. This is my favourite recipe, but I suggest, after trying it, you experiment, using port or sherry, beer or cider instead of wine and brandy. And if you wish to try the frothy version, pour the milk and cream or cream on its own in a thin stream into the bowl from a height, whisking all the time and scooping off the formed froth into dishes for serving.

2 large lemons
¼ pt (125 ml/½ cup) dry white wine
4 tbsp (60 ml/¼ cup) brandy
4 oz (100 g/½ firmly packed cup) granulated sugar
½ pt (284 ml/1¼ cups) double cream (heavy cream)

Thinly pare the rind from the lemons, inspecting each piece and removing any white pith which might have come off the lemons with the rind. Put the rinds in a large bowl. Squeeze out and strain the lemon juice into the bowl. Add the wine, brandy and sugar, cover the bowl and leave it overnight for the sugar to dissolve. Next day, remove the lemon rinds and pour in the cream. Whisk very slowly using a balloon whisk and continue until thick, slowing down as this happens because it is easy to overbeat the cream and produce a grainy texture. Turn the syllabub into small glasses, chill it and serve it with a rich shortbread.

Junket   *serves 2–4*

Junket used to be sold daily in the London streets; nowadays it is scorned as 'invalid' food, but made properly with plain bottled rennet instead of flavoured rennet powders, junket can be deliciously subtle. To this basic recipe you can add cream, thick or clotted, spreading it over the set junket before serving. If you wish to flavour the junket, stir 2 tsp (10 ml/2 tsp) brandy or rum into the warm milk or sprinkle a little ground nutmeg or cinnamon over the top. Castor sugar strewn over a junket adds a crunchy texture to the smoothness of the pudding.

1 pt (550 ml/2½ cups) milk
1 tbsp (15 ml/1 tbsp) castor sugar
1 tsp (5 ml/1 tsp) plain rennet
1 or 2 bay leaves

Warm the milk to blood heat, testing the temperature by putting a clean finger into the milk which should feel neither hot nor cold. Stir in the sugar, rennet and bay leaves and pour the mixture into a basin. Sprinkle the top with spice if desired and leave it in a warm room for 30 minutes or until it has set. Serve with cream or jam or finish the junket in any of the ways described above.

The important thing is that the milk must not boil, nor should it have boiled, because the junket will not set; however it is also worth remembering to leave a junket undisturbed while it sets, otherwise it may curdle and separate.

Eggs and Poultry

With a few chickens scratching round the door, collecting eggs might well have been a hide-and-seek game and, although smaller than those we buy now, they must have had a different flavour. The chickens, too, when past their usefulness and consigned to the pot, would have required long, slow cooking, but, again, the flavour must have been worth it.

In our quest for larger eggs and chickens we have lost something, and this is easily demonstrated the first time you taste a free-range egg, lightly boiled, or roast a free-range chicken.

However, there's a catch in the term 'free-range'. Rarely these days does it mean what it says. Larger eggs, slightly dirty and with the odd feather attached should indicate eggs from a chicken which has been trotting about freely, rather than battery-reared, but as it is difficult to buy such a chicken, I wonder where all these eggs come from. 'Free-range' often means fresh not frozen, although the chicken is still battery-reared.

You have to find a good butcher, explain in detail that you want a free-range bird in the true meaning of the term and trust him to get you the right product. You can be sure as soon as you taste.

Factory-farming of chickens and now turkeys has reduced these birds to an everyday meat with little to recommend it, watery and flavourless from being eviscerated while still warm and frozen without hanging.

But the goose is still the bird it was and for the last few years, I have cooked one for Christmas. The rich, dark meat is full of flavour and the goose grease is greeted every time with delight. It means three months of wonderful pastry.

Preserving eggs

My mother always had a bucket of eggs preserved in waterglass on the floor of the pantry. I hated having to examine each egg to ensure the shell was free of cracks and dirt before putting them into the bucket. It was a cold job because the bucket was not to be moved, and so a fresh batch of eggs would only be preserved if I crouched on the stone floor. The eggs were kept for a maximum of 12 months, and at the end of that time, the waterglass was used to scrub the floor and shelves of the pantry. Waterglass can be bought from chemists today (try Boots, who will order it if they do not have it in stock) and it must be made up according to the directions on the tin. Mother used a stone crock, but any stoneware container will do provided it is not too broad at the top which allows the waterglass to evaporate too quickly. As many as one hundred eggs may be put into any one container if they are well covered by the waterglass. Today this is only worth trying if you can buy cheap eggs and have the space to keep them. Eggs may also be preserved in salt, dried first in the oven. Pour a deep layer of salt into a pail or crock, arrange the eggs pointed ends down, and fill the spaces between with salt. A good layer of salt must be poured on top. A third method involves excluding air from the shells with fat, but this is more difficult as care must be taken to cover every bit of each egg. Melted dripping, lard or butter can be used, so can paraffin wax. Eliza Acton's method was even more time-consuming, involving painting each egg with gum arabic, coating half and letting it dry before completing the painting.

Pickled eggs are more acceptable as a preserve; frequently seen in pubs these days. If you wish to pickle eggs, make sure they are a few days old before boiling them. The white adheres to the shell of too-fresh eggs and when peeled, look more like small moonscapes than hard-boiled eggs. Boil the eggs for 10 minutes only, then cool quickly under cold running water. Boil some malt vinegar and scald a wide-necked jar. Shell the eggs, pack them into the jar and cover them with the hot vinegar. After three weeks they will be a tasty accompaniment to bread and cheese, cold meats and other pickles, but if you leave them longer they improve daily.

Recently I baked some eggs in wood ashes at the side of the fire in the dining-room to reconstruct the method by which eggs were cooked most often before the fifteenth and sixteenth centuries. Coal ash is too fierce a heat so unless you burn wood in great open fires as we do, this is some-thing you will have to miss. Timing is the difficulty, but as I find it almost impossible to time a perfectly boiled egg because the shells are so thin these days, my wood-ash baked eggs were no more disastrously over- or under-cooked than my boiled eggs. They didn't taste noticeably different, it just seemed so because of the pleasure of the unusual cooking method.

Another very old recipe uses marigold petals in egg custard. This one comes from an old hand-written recipe book I have dating back to the early eighteenth century.

Apple marigold custard   *serves 4*

4 oz (100 g/1 cup) plain flour (all purpose flour)
2 oz (50 g/¼ cup) unsalted butter
1 large cooking apple
2 large eggs, size 2
¼ pt (142 ml/⅔ cup) double cream (heavy cream)
¾ oz (20 g/1 cup) marigold petals
2 oz (50 g/¼ firmly packed cup) castor sugar

Sift the flour into a bowl and cut and rub in the butter. Mix to a stiff dough with cold water. Roll the pastry on a lightly floured board and use to line a 7 in (18 cm) shallow baking tin or flan ring standing on a baking sheet. Peel, core and thinly slice the apple and arrange the slices in the base of the pastry case. Whisk the eggs with the cream, adding the marigold petals and sugar and whisking again. Unless you have been spraying your flowers with insecticide and unless your garden is in a very built-up area, subject to petrol and diesel fumes, simply shake the flowers and pull off the petals, after checking them for insects. Otherwise, rinse the flowers first taking care to dry them completely before using the petals if the custard is not to be thinned by the water on the flowers. Bake the custard in a moderately hot oven at 400°F (200°C), gas mark 6 for 35 to 40 minutes or until it is set. Eat either hot or cold.

Pancakes, batters and fritters

Medieval books mention batters, and not just English cookbooks. Batters seem to have been the first take-away food, inexpensive to make, quick to cook, convenient to carry and tasty to eat. Look through regional cookery books of this country and you will see pancakes, fritters and batters in many different guises, each region claiming a distinct version as its own. In Ireland, it was natural to combine the potato, universally grown and relied on when it was realized how well it would grow in the moist peaty soil, with batters to make a potato pancake; in the fruit areas of Kent and the Vale of Evesham, cherries or soft fruits combine with batters to make a dish we call *clafoutis* and think of as French, while in Tewkesbury, fruity batters are cooked on saucers, or you will find plain saucer batters sandwiched with fruit and served as a convenient sweet package.

Nottingham, the home of the Bramley apple, combines whole cored apples with batter, like a sweet toad-in-the-hole, while batters were steamed in pudding basins in Victoria's days, and dressed with a fruit sauce before being sent to the table. Cooks made hasty puddings, a title which not only gives an indication of the speed with which they can be made, but shows too that these batters were a stand-by, a last resort, a dish which could be put together with ingredients always to hand even when there was little else in the kitchen.

Sweet or savoury food which is to be deep-fried needs a protective coating of batter. You can use a thick Yorkshire pudding batter or one made with milk but these make rather dense coatings. If a lighter batter is required, then use the fritter batter 1 recipe where the eggs are separated and the whites whisked and folded in just as you are ready to use the batter. Lighter and crisper still are batters made with yeast, see the fritter batter 2 recipe. Fritters can be made from fruit, apple rings, bananas, pineapple rings, or from pieces of meat, fish or poultry, cut small. Vegetables are particularly good deep-fried in a crisp coating. Try mushrooms, courgette slices, pieces of cauliflower, aubergine slices (salted, steeped, rinsed and dried first) or onion rings.

Batters

This modern batter recipe can be used with sweet or savoury additions.

4 large eggs, size 2
½ pt (300 ml/1¼ cups) milk
4 oz (100 g/1 cup) plain flour (all purpose flour)

Separate the eggs and whisk the yolks with the milk, gradually beating in the sifted flour. Leave this batter to stand until you are ready to use it, or for a maximum of 1 hour. Finally whisk the egg whites until stiff but not dry, fold them into the batter and use it at once.

For a savoury dish, season the batter with salt and pepper, finely chopped herbs such as parsley and thyme or a small pinch of dried herbs, although I would rather leave it free of herbs than use dried ones. Pour the batter over freshly fried sausages, small meat balls fried hot and just golden (they do not need to be completely cooked) or a mixture of chopped ingredients such as courgette slices, peas, sweetcorn, chopped bacon, mushrooms, or whatever you have in the store cupboard.

For puddings, pour it over stoned cherries or plums, rhubarb, apples or topped and tailed gooseberries. In all cases, use a shallow tin and cook

the batter in a moderately hot oven at 400°F (200°C), gas mark 6 for 35 to 45 minutes. Send a sweet batter to the table immediately it is cooked, sprinkled thickly with brown sugar and dotted with butter. Spice, of course, is a good addition, as is dried fruit.

Steaming a batter pudding is a tricky operation. How do you serve the pudding when it is just set without constantly removing the covers to check, or without over-cooking it to the point of leatheriness? As a rough guide, batter made with 1 pt (600 ml/2½ cups) of milk requires about 1½ hours steaming when it is robust enough to stand a quick removal of the covers for checking. Moulded batters are not the most attractive of puddings. They need a coating of sauce for decoration. Serve with additional sauce in a jug.

Pancakes

This is the basic recipe to be served with sugar and lemon, jam, honey, ice cream or fruit, or to be used with a savoury filling.

4 oz (100 g/1 cup) plain flour (all purpose flour)
Small pinch of salt
1 large egg, size 2
½ pt (300 ml/1¼ cups) milk

Sift the flour and salt into a bowl. Break the egg into a well in the flour and begin to mix by drawing the flour from the edges gradually into the egg. Add milk gradually and continue to gather in the flour, beating all the time to make a smooth batter. This amount will make about 8 pancakes which should be fried in an 8 in (20 cm) pan with a little hot lard. Pour some batter into the greased pan, tilt the pan to allow the batter to run over the base in a thin even coat, then cook the pancake for about 1 minute until it is golden brown underneath. Toss or turn it and cook for another minute until the second side is also golden. Ideally pancakes should be served hot out of the pan, but they are an anti-social pudding, particularly for the cook who makes her pancake from the last drops of batter, sitting down when everyone else is thinking about the coffee.

Pancakes will be lighter in texture if you separate the egg, beating the yolk into the flour with the milk to make the batter, then folding in the whisked egg white. Welsh, Scottish and Irish recipes use buttermilk which makes a lighter pancake and the recipe for Crempog (Welsh pancakes, small tea-time ones rather like Scotch pancakes) includes a little bicarbonate of soda.

Fritter batter 1

2 oz (50 g/½ cup) plain flour (all purpose flour)
A pinch of salt

1 level tsp (5 ml/1 level tsp) icing sugar
4 tbsp (60 ml/5 tbsp) warm water
2 tsp (10 ml/good 2 tsp) melted butter or light oil
1 egg white, size 2 or 3

Sift the flour, salt and icing sugar into a bowl and gradually mix in the warm water and melted butter or oil to make a smooth batter. Whisk the egg white until it is stiff and fold it into the batter. The first part of the batter can be made an hour or so before you want to use it, but whisk the egg white and fold it in only when you have heated the pan of oil and are ready to fry the food. Use this sweet batter for fruit fritters.

Fritter batter 2

4 oz (100 g/1 cup) plain strong flour (bread flour)
A good pinch of salt
¼ oz (7 g/1 tbsp) fresh yeast or ½ this quantity of dried yeast
¼ pt (125 ml/⅔ cup) lukewarm milk
2 eggs, size 3

Sift the flour and salt into a bowl. Cream fresh yeast in a cup using a teaspoon and add a little of the lukewarm milk to ease the creaming. Sprinkle dried yeast on top of the lukewarm milk and leave it for 15 minutes until it has formed a spongy mass on top. Make a well in the centre of the flour, pouring the fresh yeast liquid and remaining warm milk or the dried yeast liquid into the well. Separate the eggs and add the yolks to the bowl and mix to a batter with a wooden spoon. Mix well, but if there are a few lumps in the batter, it does not matter. Cover the bowl with a tea towel wrung out in hot water and leave the bowl in a warm place for about 1 hour or until the batter is covered in bubbles and looks spongy. Whisk the egg whites stiffly and fold them into the batter. Cover the bowl again and leave the batter to rise for another hour; longer will not harm.

Use the batter for either sweet or savoury foods. It is particularly good for fish, producing a light, crisp and fluffy coating, which is soft inside.

A very good pancake, like a Scotch pancake, is also made from this batter. Pour small amounts into greased frying pans, swirling each amount with the point of a spoon to form a good shape (it will not run all over the pan as a plain batter does). Fry it until golden brown on both sides. Serve with sweet or savoury toppings.

Yorkshire pudding

You will have noticed that a Yorkshire pudding and a pancake batter can be one and the same thing, although for lightness, my Yorkshire kin always insist on using measure for measure of water and milk for mixing. The secret of a Yorkshire pudding is the heat of the oven and the heat of the lard or dripping in the tin. Turn the oven up to very hot at 450°F (230°C), gas mark 8 and put the Yorkshire pudding tin(s), including small knobs of lard or dripping, in the oven as you turn it on, so that it (they) become smoking hot before pouring in the batter. Remove the tin(s) with an oven cloth, pour in the batter, return the tin(s) quickly to the oven and cook the batter for 10 to 15 minutes for small ones, 20 to 25 minutes for a large pudding.

Roast lemon chicken   *serves 6–8*

6 lb (3 kg/6 lb) chicken
Stuffing, see pages 91 and 92
1 large lemon

2 oz (50 g/4 tbsp) butter
Salt and pepper

Wipe the chicken inside and out and reserve the giblets for gravy, see page 83. Choose a stuffing and use it to plump out the breast, pushing it into a good shape, then securing the neck skin either under the trussing strings, or skewering it underneath the bird but do not pull it too tight because the stuffing expands during cooking. Prick the lemon thoroughly with a fork and push it into the body cavity. Spread the butter all over the breast, season the chicken with salt and pepper and put it on a grid in a roasting tin. Cover the breast with butter papers and roast the chicken in a moderately hot oven at 400°F (200°C), gas mark 6 for 20 minutes to each 1 lb (450 g/1 lb) plus another 15 minutes. Remove the butter papers for the last 30 minutes and let the breast brown.

Remove the chicken on to a hot serving plate while you make the gravy.

Chicken casserole with prunes   *serves 4–6*

Chickens which went into the pot used to be old fowls, past their usefulness as egg layers. Tough but tasty, they required long, slow cooking. Today chicken requires less cooking but more flavouring ingredients.

3 lb (1½ kg/3 lb) chicken
Salt and pepper
Ground mace
2 oz (50 g/4 tbsp) butter
3 large or 6 small onions
6 medium leeks
Sprigs of tarragon
Chicken stock
8 oz (225 g/2 cups) plump, juicy prunes
½ oz (15 g/2 tbsp) cornflour (cornstarch)

Wipe the chicken inside and out and leave it whole or cut it into 4 joints. Season the chicken with salt and pepper and ground mace. Fry the chicken in the butter for 5 to 10 minutes, turning it until golden on all sides. Skin the onions, leaving small ones whole but cutting larger onions in half or quarters. Remove the roots and damaged leaf tops from the leeks, cut the leeks into 4 in (10 cm) lengths and if clean, leave them whole, rinsing them well. If black loamy soil has worked its way between the leaves, then you will have to slice each leek lengthways in order to wash them thoroughly. Drain well and put them in a deep casserole dish with the onions and tarragon sprigs. Put the chicken on top and pour in enough stock to just cover the chicken. Cover the dish with the lid or with tin foil and cook the chicken in a moderate oven at 350°F (180°C), gas mark 4 for about 30 minutes, before adding the prunes. Blend the cornflour (cornstarch) with a little cold water, stir it into the stock and while doing so, taste the stock for seasoning and add more salt, pepper, mace and tarragon if you wish. Return the casserole, covered, to the oven and continue cooking for another 40 minutes to 1 hour until tender.

Chicken pie 1 *serves 4*

Mrs Glasse's recipe 'To make a chicken pie' includes nutmeg and mace, forcemeat of veal, suet, breadcrumbs, anchovy, lemon and thyme. She adds sweetbreads, some truffles and morels, 2 or 3 artichoke bottoms, a few cockscombs, a palate boiled tender, all covered with a good puff crust. Chickens Chiringrate are equally fancy; well-seasoned with forcemeat, larded with bacon, and truffles, morels and sweetbreads cut small are added. She notes that 'it will be a very high dish', and no doubt 'suitable for a great deal of company'. Maria Rundell in her cookbook, *A New System of Domestic Cookery*, 1810, gives a recipe for a veal (or chicken and parsley) pie which I give here. It is simple, but delightfully so.

3 lb (1½ kg/3 lb) chicken
Salt and pepper
2 large bunches of parsley
Milk
6 oz (150 g/1½ cups) plain flour (all purpose flour)
1½ oz (40 g/3 tbsp) lard
1½ oz (40 g/3 tbsp) butter
¼ pt (142 ml/⅔ cup) double cream (heavy cream)

Cut the chicken meat off the bones in large pieces, pulling off and discarding the skin. Put all the small pieces of chicken, winkled out of the crevices with a small sharp knife, to one side, seasoning them, as well as the large pieces of meat, with salt and pepper. Remove the parsley leaves from the stalks, put them in a basin and pour on freshly boiling water. Drain and refresh the parsley under running cold water, drain again, squeeze it dry in an old tea towel and chop it fairly finely. Layer the meat and parsley in an oval pie dish, beginning with parsley and using the small pieces of chicken first, finishing with a good layer of best meat. Pour in enough milk to come about halfway up the dish. Sift the flour into a large bowl with a good pinch each of salt and pepper. Cut and rub in the lard and butter and mix to a stiff dough with cold water. Knead the pastry lightly until it is smooth, then roll it on a lightly floured board until it is at least 2 in (5 cm) larger than the pie dish. Grease the edge of the dish, then cut off a 1 in (2.5 cm) strip around the pastry and press it on the rim of the dish, cutting and joining it neatly. Moisten this strip with water, cover the dish with the pastry and press the edges gently to seal them. Trim and decorate them. Bake the pie in a moderately hot oven at 400°F (200°C), gas mark 6 for 1 hour, covering the pastry with a piece of greaseproof paper when it has browned enough. When the chicken is cooked, cut the crust free of the dish and remove it carefully. Pour off some of the liquid, then heat the cream and pour it into the pie. Gently replace the crust and serve at once.

Chicken pie 2   *serves 4–6*

This recipe can be used for rabbit, game, veal and ham or a mixture of different meats, including sausagemeat and stuffing mixtures for extra flavour. But they should be dry, not swimming in stock or gravy. Provided you use the specified quantity of meat, you can experiment with different combinations of ingredients.

1½ lb (675 g/1½ lb) chicken meat, some in large pieces
8 oz (225 g/8 oz) good sausagemeat
4 oz (100 g/4 oz) prepared stuffing
Salt and pepper
12 oz (375 g/3 cups) plain flour (all purpose flour)
3 oz (75 g/6 tbsp) margarine
3 oz (75 g/6 tbsp) lard
2 large eggs, size 2
¼ pt (125 ml/⅔ cup) milk

Cut the chicken meat off the bones; it may be raw or cooked, but cooked is preferable because this is a fine way of using the meat stripped off the carcass. Divide the sausagemeat and stuffing into 2 or 3 pieces, depending on the quantity you have. Season the meats with salt and pepper, but keep them separate.

Sift the flour with ½ level tsp (2.5 ml/½ level tsp) salt into a bowl and rub in the margarine and lard. Mix to a stiff dough with cold water. Reserve a quarter of the dough for the lid and roll another quarter into a round slightly larger than the base of an 8 in (20 cm) loose-bottomed cake tin, using the base as a guide. Put the base in position in the tin. Roll the large piece to fit the sides and put it in position, sticking it to the base with water. Neaten the join around the base and trim and neaten the join in the large piece, again sticking it with cold water. Smooth all these joins. Layer the meat, sausagemeat and stuffing into the pastry case, roll the reserved quarter for the lid and stick it in place with water, trimming and decorating the edges. Make a central hole, keeping it open during cooking with a small tube made of rolled tin foil. Lightly beat the eggs and use a little to brush the top of the pie.

Cook the pie in a moderately hot oven at 400°F (200°C), gas mark 6 for 10 minutes to set the pastry, then whisk the milk into the remaining beaten egg, season it with salt and pepper, and pour it through the central hole, using a small funnel or a cone made of tin foil. Return the pie to the oven for another 40 or 45 minutes' cooking until the crust is a good golden brown, removing the pie from the tin towards the end of the cooking to brown the sides.

If the meat is raw, cook the pie for 20 minutes as above, then lower the temperature to moderate at 350°F (180°C), gas mark 4 and continue cooking for another 1 to 1½ hours, depending on the meat used. Cover the pie with greaseproof paper when the top is brown enough and pour in the egg mixture 40 minutes before the end of the cooking time so that it will set without curdling.

Cooking turkey

Turkey is my least favourite poultry. Generally it is too dry a meat, although the British Turkey Federation cooked a turkey dinner that proved how good it can be. The trend nowadays is to self-basting turkeys and turkeys injected with chicken stock for additional flavour because today's housewife expects to strip off the wrappings, put the meat in the oven and after the simplest roasting, find it wonderfully tasty. I do not think that there is any substitute for the flavours to be added with stuffings, good gravies, careful cooking and by choosing fresh produce in preference to frozen. Having to cook turkey occasionally, I looked for the best way of producing moist meat and find this method, given to me by a great friend, Mrs K., perfect. (Incidentally, my friend is not coyly preserving her anonymity; for the last ten years, I have shortened her name to the initial only.) My friend collects the giblets with her turkey, puts them in a large pan of water with flavourings such as onions, parsley, bay leaves, celery, peppercorns, thyme sprigs and carrot and cooks the giblets for 15 to 30 minutes. The contents of the pan are then poured into the meat tin, a grid is put in the tin and the turkey sits on top, out of the stock but steaming in the flavoured heat. It is moist and tender when cooked and the stock is made for the gravy without using extra heat.

Most chickens which have been frozen suffer from too much moisture so this method will not do.

Roast turkey   *serves 8–12*

If you prefer a more conventional method of roasting the turkey, this is the one to use. It includes instructions for calculating the cooking time for any size of bird.

12 lb (5½ kg/12 lb) turkey
Stuffing, see pages 91 and 92
4 oz (100 g/½ cup) butter
Salt and pepper

Wipe the turkey inside and out, removing the giblets and using them to make stock, see page 33. Choose a stuffing from pages 91 and 92 and use it to fill the cavity of the bird. If you buy a turkey complete with its head, you can remove the neck skin to make the stuffed turkey neck pâté described below. Spread the butter all over the breast and arrange the turkey on a grid in the roasting tin on its side, that is with the underside exposed to the heat. Cover the turkey with a large piece of heavy tin foil, tucking it under the rim of the meat tin.

Calculate the cooking time on the combined weight of turkey and stuffing and allow 15 minutes per 1 lb (450 g/1 lb) for anything up to 14 lb (6½ kg/14 lb) and over this weight, allow 25 minutes to each 1 lb (450 g/ 1 lb). This weight of bird will cook in just under 3½ hours.

Put the bird into a moderately hot oven at 375°F (190°C), gas mark 5 and after 1½ hours cooking, turn the turkey over, on to the other breast. For the last 45 minutes, turn the turkey on to its back, breast upwards, remove the tin foil and let it brown. This method ensures evenly cooked meat; the legs are tender without the breast becoming overdone.

Stuffed turkey neck   *serves 4–6*

Jane Grigson gives this recipe in *English Food* (Macmillan, 1974). I have not found the recipe in any of my old cookery books, nor in my researches in libraries, but Mrs Grigson suggests that Poddyng of Capoun necke (1430) is the original reference. Since reading her book, I have tried the recipe several times, altering it according to what ingredients were to hand, but I think her version is still the best and I repeat it here.

1 capon, goose or turkey neck
8 oz (225 g/8 oz) high-quality sausagemeat
1 heaped tbsp (20 ml/2 tbsp) finely chopped parsley
2 egg yolks, size 2 or 3
Ground mace
Ground cloves   *A pinch of saffron stamens (optional)*
Salt and pepper   *The liver of the bird*

For this pudding you must buy your poultry complete with the head and using scissors cut the skin around the neck as close to the breast as you can manage and as close to the beak as possible. Then cut the skin up the neck from breast to beak so that it can be peeled off in one piece. Lay it on a work surface skin side down.

Mix the sausagemeat with the parsley, egg yolks and ground mace, cloves and salt and pepper to taste. If you are using the saffron, steep the stamens in a very little hot water for 5 or 10 minutes, then strain the liquid into the sausagemeat when it is a good colour. Cut the liver of the bird into 2 or 3 large pieces. Spread the sausagemeat mixture on the neck skin, lay the pieces of liver on top, then moisten your hands and work the sausagemeat up from the sides on top of the liver to enclose it completely, but still keeping the oblong shape. Fold the skin over to enclose the filling and put the roll, cut side down, into a small loaf tin. Bake it in the oven with the bird or if more convenient, roast it in a moderate oven at 350°F (180°C), gas mark 4 for about 45 minutes until it is slightly brown on top. Serve it cut into slices, hot or cold, although the flavour is better if you keep it in a cool place for a day or so before cutting it.

If you do not use the giblets for gravy or if you simply boil them for stock and then discard them, consider them for this pudding. Chop them into small pieces, raw or cooked, removing the flesh from the neck bones and cutting away greenish bits from the stomach.

Roast duck with grapefruit   *serves 4*

6 lb (2¾ kg/6 lb) duck
4 large grapefruit
1 level tsp (5 ml/1 good tsp) arrowroot (cornstarch)
1 level tsp (5 ml/1 good tsp) castor sugar
Salt and pepper

Wipe the duck inside and out, removing the giblets and reserving them for soup. Put the duck on a shelf towards the top of the oven with a meat tin underneath it, on a lower shelf, to catch the drips. Roast the duck in a moderately hot oven at 400°F (200°C), gas mark 6 for 2 hours or 20 minutes per 1 lb (450 g/1 lb) if you have a larger bird. When cooked, transfer it to a serving dish and keep it hot.

Squeeze and strain the juice from 2 grapefruit while the duck cooks and cut all the peel and pith off the others, slicing the flesh into ½ in (1.25 cm) rounds. If the grapefruit are large, it is better to cut individual segments free from the skins. Blend the grapefruit juice with the arrowroot (cornstarch) and sugar. Drain off all the fat from the meat tin, leaving only the juices and sediment. Stir the grapefruit juice into the tin and bring it slowly to the boil on top of the stove, stirring all the time that the sauce is thickening. Stir in the grapefruit slices or segments and let them

heat through for 2 or 3 minutes. Season with salt and pepper and pour this sauce over the duck to serve. Or, if you prefer, scoop some of the grapefruit pieces from the sauce and use them for garnish, serving the sauce in a sauceboat.

Roast goose   *serves 6*

The goose has always been the bird for festivals, supplanted largely by the turkey brought to this country from the Americas after Columbus's discovery. Fattened on gleaned corn, geese were served for harvest or Michaelmas feasting, often with pieces of rabbit cooked inside them. The drier rabbit meat absorbed some of the goose fat. Another method of cooking the two meats was roasting the rabbit in the goose drippings, popular because it eked out the goose meat and provided a goose-flavoured but slightly less rich dinner for those who preferred it. The only way to cook this dish now that we have no spits and open fires, is to put the goose on the oven shelf, the rabbit joints on the shelf below and a large meat tin below again to catch the goose drippings after they have basted the rabbit joints.

8 lb (3½ kg/8 lb) goose
Approximately 12 oz (325 g/3 cups) stuffing, see pages 91 and 92
1 lb (450 g/1 lb) rabbit portions
Salt and pepper

Wipe the goose inside and out, and if the butcher has not done this for you pull out handfuls of the soft white fat from the breast, putting it in the roasting tin. Prick the skin thoroughly with a fork. Prepare the stuffing, using a tart mixture such as chopped apples soaked in a little cider or chopped onions mixed with fresh sage and a few breadcrumbs. Wipe the rabbit portions and use leg joints whole but cut the meat from the bones of other pieces. Spread a good thick layer of stuffing inside the goose, then arrange the rabbit pieces on top, finally covering them with the remaining stuffing. Skewer or sew the skin together to hold in the stuffing. Stand the bird on a rack (the grid from the grill pan) in the roasting tin and cook it in a moderately hot oven at 400°F (200°C), gas mark 6 for 20 minutes to each 1 lb (450 g/1 lb) plus another 20 minutes, calculating the cooking time on the combined weight of the goose and the stuffings. Do not baste the goose during cooking; it has enough fat of its own which will run down the breast as it roasts. Pour off the fat once or twice during cooking, depending on the depth of the meat tin, and when the goose is done, serve it with a good gravy and a sharp apple sauce.

Goose grease

You will collect something like 3½ pt (2 1/4¼ pt) of grease during the cooking which you can freeze or keep in the refrigerator. Use it to make wonderfully short light pastry for savoury pies. In some areas, goose grease is still eaten on bread seasoned only with salt and pepper, in much the same way that beef dripping makes a savoury topping for bread or toast for tea time. But its uses were legion; a much-treasured grease for poultices, keeping leather supple, greasing dairy equipment for smooth rust-free running, preventing chapping of farm labourers' hands and cows' udders alike, and as a polish to prevent cracked hoofs and to shine trotters, hoofs, beaks and horns of animals going on show.

Vegetables

It seems a pity that we treat vegetables so badly, submerging them in water, adding bicarbonate of soda to improve the colour but destroying the Vitamin C content in the process, and once they are overcooked and limp, serving them plainly. It is surprising that more people do not refuse their greens.

Gradually we are learning to cook our vegetables lightly. The Chinese take-away is to be thanked for introducing us to the stir-fry method of cooking and meals containing crisp, barely cooked bean sprouts, shavings of carrots, succulent pieces of onion, leek and cabbage.

The older vegetable recipes in English cookery show that at one time we prepared and cooked vegetables in many different ways, now largely replaced by a country-wide boiling.

Considering that in the past much of England was a market garden, everyone having his patch of ground on which to grow potatoes, onions and leeks, the English favourites, it is strange that now we discover the true taste of fresh-grown vegetables only when war or other economic necessity makes us dig up the lawn and plant them. It is the Italians who showed us how much could be achieved in the vegetable garden and it is the Continent we must thank for new and improved varieties: Belgium for chicory, the French court for its devotion to the globe artichoke and its introduction of it to England, and Holland for the better cabbages; our indigenous varieties being loose-leafed mop-headed plants like the kale. But except for the cabbage, these vegetables do not belong in English rural cookery; instead, recipes for parsnips, leeks, mushrooms, pease pudding and the many dishes cooked from the potato.

Leek soup   *serves 4–6*

It would be nonsense to suggest that the English did not make soups simply because there are no recipes which are traditional; unlike the cawl of Wales and Scotch broth and cullen skink of Scotland. The truth is probably quite simple. The soups which were made were probably simply boiled vegetables, occasionally eked out with a little meat. Because the north-east of England is such a traditional leek-growing area, cooks must have made them into a soup, although it took the French to marry them with potatoes, chill the result and give us vichyssoise.

1 large onion
2 lb (1 kg/2 lb) leeks
2 large potatoes
2 oz (50 g/¼ cup) butter
1¾ pt (1 l/4½ cups) chicken stock

2 egg yolks, size 2 (optional)
1 level tbsp (15 ml/1 good tbsp)
*   finely chopped parsley*
Salt and pepper

Skin and finely chop the onion. Remove damaged leaves and roots from the leeks and roughly slice the leeks across into rounds. Wash well to remove any soil which collects in the tightly packed leaves. Peel and roughly chop the potatoes. Melt the butter in a large pan and fry the onion gently for 3 minutes, then add the potato and leeks and continue to fry gently for another 5 minutes, stirring occasionally. Pour in the stock, season with salt and white pepper and bring to the boil. Cover the pan and simmer the soup for 30 minutes, or until the vegetables are tender. Liquidize the soup until it is smooth then return the purée to a clean saucepan and check the seasoning. Enrich if liked with the egg yolks, stir in the parsley and reheat gently without letting the soup boil. Serve with toast croûtons.

Bubble and squeak   *serves 2–3*

When Monday meant a long, steamy day at the copper washing the week's clothes, meals were simple, and bubble and squeak or similar fried dishes, consisting of what was left from Sunday's roast meal, were popular. They involved no shopping, little preparation and cooking, leaving all a housewife's energy free for achieving a white wash, a snowy, billowing line of laundry. Colcannon is Ireland's version.

8 oz (225 g/8 oz) leanest, pinkest roast meat
Beef dripping
8 oz (225 g/8 oz) cooked cabbage
8 oz (225 g/8 oz) cooked, mashed potatoes
Gravy
Salt and pepper

Obviously the quantities should be adjusted to suit what you have, the above amounts supplying a hearty meal for 2 or 3 people. Cut the meat into even-sized pieces then melt a large knob of dripping in a frying pan and when it is really hot, add the cabbage and potatoes, mixing and mashing them well in the pan. Add the meat pieces and some gravy to moisten and season well, then form the mixture into a cake. Fry it until the bottom is golden brown and crisp when it should be slid from the pan on to a plate and flipped over off the plate back into the pan so that the other side can brown. You may have to add a little more dripping, so make sure it is smoking hot again otherwise too much is absorbed by the potatoes. Reshape the cake if necessary. Cut into wedges and serve very hot.

Cauliflower cake   *serves 4*

This is a dish which can be made with a variety of vegetables; sprouts and cabbage are as successful as cauliflower.

1 small cauliflower
Salt and pepper
½ pt (250 ml/1¼ cups) milk
1 oz (25 g/2 tbsp) butter
4 oz (100 g/1¼ firmly packed cups) fresh white breadcrumbs
2 oz (50 g/4 tbsp) grated Cheddar cheese
2 large eggs, size 2
Ground nutmeg
Toasted breadcrumbs

Cut the cauliflower into small sprigs, rinse them and cook them in boiling salted water for 3 minutes. Heat the milk, stir in the butter and bread-crumbs and when they have swollen, stir in the cheese and season the mixture well with salt and plenty of freshly ground white pepper. Sepa-rate the eggs and beat the yolks into the pan then gently cook the mixture for 2 minutes, stirring all the time. Stir in the cauliflower sprigs, keeping them whole. Whisk the egg whites until they are stiff and fold them into the mixture.

Turn the mixture into a greased 6 in (15 cm) cake tin with a fixed base after sprinkling the base and sides with the toasted breadcrumbs. Cook it in a moderately hot oven at 400°F (200°C), gas mark 6 for 25 to 30 minutes or until it is firm. Turn out to serve.

Braised celery   *serves 4*

1 unsmoked streaky bacon rasher
1 oz (25 g/2 tbsp) butter
1 medium onion
2 heads of celery
½ pt (250 ml/1¼ cups) good stock
1 level tsp (5 ml/1 good tsp) finely chopped fresh parsley
½ level tsp (2.5 ml/½ good tsp) finely chopped fresh thyme
A good pinch of ground mace
Salt and pepper

Cut the rind from the rasher and chop the bacon roughly. Fry it until the fat runs freely, then add the butter. Skin and finely chop the onion, add it to the pan and cook it with the bacon for 5 to 8 minutes until it softens and begins to colour. Prepare the celery, cutting off the coarse outside stalks, removing damaged leaves and the root and finally cutting the heads into 4 in (10 cm) lengths. Rinse them well, drain well, making sure there is no soil lurking down at the base between the stalks. Drain the fat from the bacon and onions and put them in a casserole. Lay the celery on top and pour in only enough stock to come a quarter of the way up the celery, that is, just covering the onions and bacon. Sprinkle with parsley, thyme and mace and plenty of salt and pepper. Put on the lid; if it does not give a good seal, cover the dish with a piece of foil then jam on the lid.

Cook the celery in a moderate oven at 325°F (160°C), gas mark 3 for 1½ hours or until it is tender. Pierce the thickest part with a small sharp knife to be certain. Drain off the stock, save it for soup, and serve the celery with the onion and bacon pieces.

Cabbage with caraway seeds   *serves 4–6*

½ *firm white cabbage*
Salt and pepper
4 oz (100 g/½ cup) unsalted butter
2 level tbsp (30 ml/2 good tbsp) caraway seeds

Remove the outer leaves from the cabbage and cut out the core. Shred the remainder fairly finely. Bring a large pan containing about 1 in (2.5 cm) of salted water to the boil, then add the cabbage and the lid and let it cook for 5 minutes until it is tender but still crisp. Drain well, then return the cabbage to the pan and chop it roughly. A saucer in a colander used to be the method; I do not think there is a better way of achieving chopped cabbage without reducing it to a mash. Add the butter, let it melt while tossing the cabbage all the time to coat every piece. Season it with salt and plenty of pepper then stir in the caraway seeds.

Red cabbage   *serves 6*

Like leeks, red cabbage seems to belong to the north, except that the northerners were less inventive with red cabbage, turning it year after year into a pickle to be served with boiled beef. A hand-written cookery book in my possession dating back to the middle of the eighteenth century has a brief mention of red cabbage stewed and the first mention after that that I have found is in Maria Rundell's *A New System of Domestic Cookery*; my copy is dated 1810. Mrs Rundell stews it plainly, adding a little vinegar and a knob of butter. I prefer to add some apple to red cabbage and often include pieces of bacon, more or less depending on whether I want a side dish or a main course supper dish.

1 lb (450 g/1 lb) unsmoked lean bacon
1 large red cabbage
4 oz (100 g/½ cup) unsalted butter
½ pt (250 ml/1¼ cups) bacon stock
Salt and pepper
Ground nutmeg
4 Cox's orange pippins

A small piece of bacon is preferable to rashers; it can be cut into even-sized chunks or even left whole to be sliced when serving. Prepare the red cabbage, trimming off damaged outer leaves then quartering it and cutting out the core. Thinly slice the cabbage and the core, if liked, but more thinly. Heat the butter in a pan and fry the bacon pieces or piece until lightly browned on all sides. Transfer them to a deep pan, put the cabbage on top, seasoning each layer with salt and pepper and nutmeg and pour in the stock. Core and slice the apples, cutting out bruises and blemishes, otherwise there is no need to peel them. Add them to the pan and cover with a lid. Simmer gently for 1 hour, checking towards the end of the cooking time that the liquid hasn't evaporated.

If you use a whole piece of bacon, remove it from the cooking pot, set it in the middle of a hot serving dish and pile the cabbage and apple around it.

Roast onions   *serves 4*

This simple dish is very tasty; it was often served for supper with bread and butter. Choose large Spanish onions for their mildness.

4 large Spanish onions
Salt and pepper
Unsalted butter

First boil the onions in their skins for about 20 minutes then drain and dry them. Enclose each onion in a piece of well-buttered foil and roast them in a moderate oven at 350°F (180°C), gas mark 4 for 1½ to 2 hours depending on their size. Like roast potatoes, when done they will feel soft if squeezed.

Remove them from their foil wraps, put each one on a plate and serve seasoned with salt and freshly ground white pepper and with unsalted butter. The best way to eat a roast onion is to season and top with knobs of butter as you cut into it, adding more as you work your way into the centre.

Fried leeks   *serves 4–6*

Simply cooked in bacon fat with a little hot water added to make a gravy, this dish was a favourite north country early evening meal. We called it tea, but it was a substantial meal, always including something savoury such as a ham salad in summer, and fish or potato cakes, leeks or fried black pudding in winter. Nowadays I prefer the following recipe for leeks, which should more properly be called stewed leeks.

1½ lb (675 g/1½ lb) leeks
4 tbsp (60 ml/5 tbsp) olive oil
1 clove of garlic
1 bay leaf
4 large tomatoes
Salt and pepper
1 tsp (5 ml/1 good tsp) lemon juice

Prepare the leeks and cut green and white parts into 1 in (2.5 cm) lengths, rinsing and draining them well. Heat the oil in a large frying pan and add the leeks. Skin and crush the garlic clove into the pan. Add the bay leaf, cover the pan, and simmer the leeks for 20 minutes. Meanwhile, drop the tomatoes into boiling water then remove the skins. Chop the tomatoes roughly, add them to the pan with plenty of salt and pepper and continue cooking for another 5 to 10 minutes, stirring occasionally and adding a little more oil if the pan is drying out. Finally taste for seasoning, stir in the lemon juice and serve.

Leek pudding   *serves 2–4*

Men of the north-east of Britain still grow leeks to mammoth sizes, entering these for prizes, but even those which take the honours aren't worth much in the pot. The renown of producing such a vegetable is enough for the grower. My father once gave me several of these gigantic but disappointing specimens. I consigned them to a homely vegetable soup using them all to make up for their lack of flavour. The medium-size fruits or vegetables are always the tastiest, most tender and delicious, and for this pudding, choose good-looking middle-aged leeks, use the white and green parts of the leaves and waste nothing.

8 oz (225 g/2 cups) self-raising flour (all purpose flour with raising agent)
Salt and pepper
4 oz (100 g/1 cup) shredded suet
8 or 10 leeks

Sift the flour into a bowl with plenty of salt and pepper. Stir in the suet thoroughly then mix to a soft but not sticky dough with cold water. Roll the pastry on a lightly floured board after cutting off one third for the pudding lid. When the pastry is rolled to a large round, lightly flour the surface and fold it in half. The easiest way to line a pudding basin is to form this half-circle of pastry into a basin shape. With the folded edge nearest to you, push each half of the fold away from you and towards each other so that you form almost a quarter-circle. The pastry will wrinkle along the rounded edge. Then take the rolling pin and roll the point to elongate it. Flour your fist, put it into the pastry bag and lift it into a greased pudding basin. Smooth the folds flat against the basin sides to form a seam-free lining.

Cut the roots and damaged and browned leaf ends from the leeks. Cut each one in half lengthways and rinse them thoroughly to remove any soil caught between the leaves. Drain well and cut into 1 in (2.5 cm) slices. Pack the pudding basin with leaves, and I do mean pack, because during cooking they break down and the harder you can press them into the basin the more full your cooked pudding will be. Season each layer of leeks well with salt and pepper. This is the traditional filling, but if you wish to make more of it, bury a bay leaf in the leeks and add some chopped and peeled tomatoes. Roll the remaining pastry into a round to fit the top of the basin then moisten the edge of the pastry lining. Put the lid in place and pinch the edge with the lining edge to form a good seal. Cover the basin with greased greaseproof paper, than add a layer of foil, pleating it under the rim of the basin or tying it on with string. Steam or boil the pudding for 2 hours then serve it hot with a good gravy, or serve the pudding as an accompaniment to a simple grill or roast meal when it will feed 6 people.

Brussels sprouts with chestnuts   *serves 6–8*

The vegetable to serve with the Christmas turkey.

1 lb (450 g/1 lb) fresh chestnuts
1 lb (450 g/1 lb) fresh sprouts
Salt and pepper
3 oz (75 g/6 tbsp) butter

Make a slit in the shell of each chestnut on the flat side using a small, sharp knife. Drop them into a pan of boiling water and boil for 3 to 6 minutes, then remove them one at a time and peel them as soon as you can handle them. They must be peeled while still hot and you should remove both the tough outer shell and the pale brown bitter skin. If any chestnuts stubbornly refuse to come free of their inner or outer skins, return them to the boiling water and boil them for a while longer.

Prepare the sprouts, choosing even-sized ones and removing outer damaged leaves, trimming the stalks and making a small cross-cut in each stalk. Cook the chestnuts in boiling salted water for about 25 minutes until they are tender then drain them and keep them hot. Cook the sprouts in boiling salted water for 10 to 12 minutes until they are just tender, still slightly crisp in the middle. Drain very well and return them to the pan with the butter and chestnuts and toss them together to coat all with butter. Season with salt and freshly ground white pepper and serve at once.

Creamed mushrooms   *serves 4*

Big horse or field mushrooms are so hard to find these days, although occasionally they do appear in the shops. These are the mushrooms to use for this recipe; they colour the sauce a purplish grey which is so attractive. Button mushrooms are less successful, lacking the flavour of horse mushrooms, but the large open caps will do and are preferable to the tight white buds of button mushrooms.

1 lb (450 g/1 lb) large horse mushrooms
4 oz (100 g/½ cup) unsalted butter
2 oz (50 g/¼ cup) plain flour (all purpose flour)
1 pt (500 ml 2½ cups) milk and cream mixed
Salt and pepper
A little lemon juice

Rinse the mushrooms only if really necessary, draining and drying them thoroughly. Field mushrooms will need peeling, cultivated mushrooms can be wiped to remove bits of the growing loam. Trim the stalks. Break the mushrooms into large, rough pieces. Heat the butter in a fairly large saucepan and fry the mushrooms for 1 or 2 minutes, then stir in the flour and cook the mixture gently for 1 minute. Gradually stir in the milk and cream, thickening the sauce on top of the stove. Season with salt and plenty of freshly ground black pepper, add a squeeze of lemon juice and serve on hot buttered toast. Dilute the mixture further with milk for a soup.

Pease pudding   *serves 4*

Tie a pease pudding mixture in a cloth, making a round ball of it, and simmer it in the pan with boiled beef and carrots, see page 69. You can add the dumplings or not as you please. This is the traditional method;

today the dried peas are cooked in a pan and then reduced to a purée, seasoned and steamed, but this makes extra pans on the stove. Both methods are useful to know.

½ lb (225 g/½ lb) dried split peas
Good beef stock
1 large egg, size 3
Salt and pepper
2 oz (50 g/4 tbsp) butter

Soak the peas for a good 4 hours in plenty of cold water if you have stored them in your cupboard for any length of time. If bought fresh and bright from a shop with a good turnover, they will not require soaking. To cook them, drain them well, put them in a pan and cover them with good beef stock in preference to plain water. Cook them for about 1 hour or until they are soft enough to purée. Drain off the stock, keeping it for soup. Mash them well, not too smooth, then mix in the egg, plenty of salt and pepper and the butter, blending well. If you wish to tie the mixture in a cloth, make sure it is fairly firm; for steaming in a buttered basin, it can be a little sloppy. Cover the basin with foil and steam or boil the mixture for about 1 hour. If cooking it in a cloth with the beef, an hour is ample. Turn it out of its basin or cloth and serve with boiled beef.

Parsnip crisps   *serves 4–6*

Instead of potato crisps, particularly with plainer meats and poultry, I cook parsnip crisps. They are no more trouble than chips and they may be served on their own as a nibble.

4 large parsnips
Oil for deep frying
Salt

Using a vegetable peeler, remove the peel from the parsnips and cut off roots and tops. Shave the roots into slivers, ignoring the cores as they are often too woody to eat. Heat the oil and cook a few pieces at a time until they are golden and crisp, then remove and drain them on crumpled kitchen paper while you fry another batch. Sprinkle them with salt.

Creamed parsnips   *serves 4*

Following the Victorian belief in the absolute perfection of British life, including our cooking, we turned full circle and became ashamed of our indigenous ingredients and traditional dishes. Now we serve mange-tout, glistening with a touch of lard, as the Chinese recipe for snow peas instructs us, narrow french beans laced with garlic and herbs, spaghetti and rice, anything except the vegetables which we grow well and cook simply. This is a perfect example.

1½ lb (675 g/1½ lb) parsnips
Salt and pepper
2 oz (50 g/4 tbsp) butter
4 tbsp (60 ml/5 tbsp) double cream (heavy cream)

Peel the parsnips, cutting off the roots and stems. Cut the vegetables into even-sized pieces and put them into cold, salted water. Bring them to the boil, then cover and cook for 20 to 25 minutes until tender when pierced with a knife blade. Older parsnips may well need more cooking. Drain well and dry by tossing them in the pan over the heat. Mash them thoroughly. A potato masher usually leaves lumps; ideally liquidize the parsnips or put them in a food processor for a second or two to make a completely smooth purée. Return the purée to the rinsed pan, season it well with salt and pepper, add the butter and cream and stir over a gentle heat until piping hot and mixed.

Mixtures of roots are often very successful. Swedes, for their colour, and turnips are a pleasing combination; so are potatoes and swedes or carrots and turnips. And you might like to try the addition of a little ground nutmeg, mace or allspice, if not in the mixture, at least as a garnish.

Game chips

Traditionally made to accompany roast game, these chips with holes in them can be made only with a mandolin, a wooden kitchen implement with a corrugated metal blade. The mandolin also has a straight blade for making plain chips.

Large potatoes
Dripping or oil for deep frying
Salt

Large potatoes are easiest to handle when cutting. Peel each one then hold each potato against the wavy blade of the mandolin with your fingers and push down to grate off a slice. This first one will be corrugated but without holes. Now turn the potato through 90° and grate again. This slice will be right, full of holes as you criss-cross the grooves of the first slice. Now turn the potato back through 90° and slice again and continue slicing, turning the potato each time. Heat the dripping or oil to 375°F (190°C). Wash the potato slices to remove some of the starch and pat each one dry with a tea towel. Lower some of the chips into the dripping or oil in a basket, fry for 2 or 3 minutes until they are golden brown, remove and drain while you fry the next batch. Serve sprinkled with salt.

Crisps, of course, are made in exactly the same way using the straight blade. They make a wonderful drinks nibble, as different in flavour from commercial crisps as home-made jam is from the bought varieties.

Pan haggarty   *serves 4–8*

Also from the north-east of England, this simple dish is a fry-up of potatoes and onions, deliciously simple, warming and tasty. There are many regional dishes which are similar and you will notice that many of the classic French potato dishes are also similar. It seems a pity that we should accept these French potato dishes as special, serving them for dinner parties, but eschew our own traditions as too basic or homely for all except family eating.

2 lb (1 kg/2 lb) potatoes
3 large onions
4 oz (100 g/4 oz) Cheddar cheese
4 oz (100 g/4 oz) good beef dripping, bacon fat or lard
Salt and pepper

Peel the potatoes and cut them into fine slices of an even thickness. Skin and coarsely grate the onions. Grate the cheese. Heat the dripping, bacon fat or lard in a large frying pan. It must be a thick and heavy pan; thin pans have little tolerance of long, slow cooking necessary to melt the potatoes into a golden tenderness. Layer the potatoes, onions and cheese into the pan, seasoning each layer with salt and pepper, freshly ground preferably. Cook the mixture very slowly on top of the stove for 30 to 45 minutes until the potatoes are completely tender, testing them by pushing a thin knife blade right through. Finally brown the potato topping under the grill for a few minutes just to fleck the top with gold.

Fish

There are no tales of British fishermen buying up delicacies off foreign coasts as there are of the French taking every Dublin Bay prawn the Irish caught, and now buying much of the monkfish we land on the shores of this country. There must be many people who have eaten only cod, and that encased in a coat of batter thicker than the fish itself and accompanied with indifferent chips from a shop. And again the chips would be better if they were cooked in dripping, rather than in cheap oil.

Herring have been overfished and therefore have vanished from our breakfast and tea tables and our prime fish is now so expensive it has ceased to be even a luxury; it is largely forgotten. Turbot, sea trout, salmon, trout, whitebait and mackerel are marvellous when fresh, less exciting after freezing has reduced their colour and flavour. Dabs have disappeared, another fish seen less and less is the eel, and, like the pike, you have to look in old cookbooks for methods of dealing with and cooking it.

However, our smoked fish continues to be supreme. Fat and oily Manx kippers, Yarmouth bloaters, Finnan haddock from Scotland (a pale creamy-coloured fish complete with backbone, not the bright yellow, dyed haddock and cod which masquerade as smoked haddock), are worth every penny of their price.

Intensive farming of fish is a modern practice, the only product which does not suffer in loss of texture and taste from factory-farming methods of rearing. Oysters and trout are two of our successes, but mussels are being cultivated in the north-west of the country and around the northern isles of Scotland, and experiments with queen scallops and lobster are in process.

If this is a rather depressing look at fish, it is because I am in despair at the trend towards thousands of tons of few varieties of fish being brought into the fishing ports, all to be consigned to the freezer. Perhaps if we were more insistent on trying different fish, more would be available for experiment. Billingsgate market, soon to be moved from its old home on the Thames in London, does sell more varieties than are seen in our fast-disappearing fish shops, but you have to be there early to beat the restaurateurs, who know a good thing, buy well, and buy all that's available.

On a more exotic note, have a look in a fishmonger's shop who specializes in fish for the immigrant population. You might not be able to shallow-fry a dab in butter, but you can cook a flying fish.

Devilled whitebait   *serves 4–6*

Whitebait were caught in great quantities in the Thames estuary and whitebait dinners became fashionable after William Pitt, the Prime Minister was invited and accepted bringing with him several members of the Government. The small fry of herrings and sprats, whitebait were a great delicacy, less so now, although good restaurants usually include them as a first course. Packets of frozen whitebait can be found in many freezer cabinets and these may be cooked as soon as they are thawed enough to separate them without damage.

2 lb (1 kg/2 lb) whitebait   *Cayenne pepper*
2 oz (50 g/½ cup) plain flour (all purpose flour)
Salt and pepper
Fat or oil for deep frying

Thaw the whitebait if they are frozen. If fresh, pick them over, discarding any that are badly damaged, then rinse the fish and drain them well. Put the flour in a large bag with a good pinch each of salt and pepper and shake the bag to mix the ingredients. Add a few whitebait at a time, shake them in the seasoned flour, then shake off any excess. Fry them a few at a time in hot fat or oil for 2 or 3 minutes, just until they are golden brown. Remove and drain and continue frying. It is best to fry in very small batches so that the fish remain separate; more than a handful will stick together in the frying. Sprinkle after draining with plenty of cayenne pepper and serve hot with lemon quarters and thin brown bread and butter.

Fish pie   *serves 6*

Any kind of white fish may be used for a fish pie and the final covering can be of your choosing. Shortcrust or puff pastry, mashed potatoes, even a savoury crumble mixture can be used.

1½ lb (675 g/1½ lb) white fish   *A good bunch of parsley*
1 pt (600 ml/2½ cups) milk   *1 large egg, size 2 or 3*
2 oz (50 g/4 tbsp) butter
2 oz (50 g/½ cup) plain flour (all purpose flour)
Salt and pepper
1½ lb (675 g/1½ lb) freshly cooked potatoes or 8 oz (225 g/8 oz) pastry

Skin the fish and cut it into convenient pieces. Put it in a pan with the milk and simmer it for 10 minutes until it is just beginning to flake. In another pan, melt the butter and stir in the flour, cooking the roux gently for 1 minute. Drain the fish, and gradually stir 1 pt (600 ml/2½ cups) of the fish liquid into the roux. Bring the sauce slowly to the boil, stirring it all the time, then simmer it for 2 or 3 minutes, stirring occasionally. Season the sauce well with salt and pepper. Finely chop the parsley leaves and stir a good handful into the sauce. Flake the fish, stir it into the sauce and turn it into a fairly deep 2½ pt (1½ l/3½ pt) pie dish.

Freshly cooked potatoes should be well mashed, seasoned with salt and pepper and enriched with the beaten egg before spreading or piping them over the fish mixture. If you wish to cover the pie with pastry, use the beaten egg to glaze it before baking.

Bake a potato-topped pie in a moderate oven at 350°F (180°C), gas mark 4 for 30 to 35 minutes or until the potato is golden brown, but put a pastry pie into a moderately hot oven 400°F (200°C), gas mark 6 and cook it for 25 to 30 minutes. Puff pastry requires a slightly hotter temperature but approximately the same cooking time.

White fish soup   *serves 6*

The English do not have a great tradition of making soups from fish. The Scots have their cullen skink made from smoked haddock and partan bree from crab, but the English seem to have confined their efforts to oysters which were once very cheap and the food of the majority. White soup recipes tend to be simple, relying on the flavour of fresh haddock or cod. I have found that a small amount of ground almonds improves the flavour considerably.

1¼ lb (550 g/1¼ lb) firm white fish such as haddock, cod, coley or hake
1 medium onion   *Salt and pepper*
A few parsley stalks   *5 or 6 white peppercorns*
2 oz (50 g/4 tbsp) unsalted butter
2 oz (50 g/½ cup) plain flour (all purpose flour)
¼ pt (142 ml/⅔ cup) double cream (heavy cream)
1 level tbsp (15 ml/1 level tbsp) ground almonds
1 level tbsp (15 ml/1 level tbsp) finely chopped parsley

Skin the fish and cut the flesh into pieces. Put it in a large pan and pour in 1¾ pt (1 l/4½ cups) cold water. Skin and roughly chop the onion and add it to the pan with the parsley stalks, 1 level tsp (5 ml/1 level tsp) salt and the peppercorns. Bring very slowly to the boil then simmer the fish for 30 minutes. Strain the fish and remove and discard any bones, the stalks, onion and peppercorns.

Melt the butter in another large pan and stir in the flour, cooking the roux gently for 1 minute. Remove the pan from the heat and gradually stir in the strained fish stock. Bring the soup to the boil if necessary then lower the heat and simmer it for 5 minutes, stirring it now and then. Add the fish, flaking it evenly beforehand then stir in the cream and ground almonds. Simmer the soup for another 5 minutes without letting it boil then check the seasoning, adding more salt if necessary and ground white pepper. Finally stir in the chopped parsley and serve.

Jellied eels

Devotees of jellied eels are often Cockneys, whether or not they live in London, in much the same way that no southerner can contemplate eating a dish of tripe, this delicacy belonging to the north. The best places for jellied eels are in the East End of London, although there is one stall on the road outside the Marquis of Granby public house at Cambridge Circus, midway down the Charing Cross Road in central London where you can buy a portion of jellied eels served from the traditional white enamel washing-up bowl. Jellied eels are not usually made at home, although once the eel has been killed and cut into 2 in (5 cm) pieces, which the fishmonger will do for you, it is easy enough to bake it with flavourings and enough vinegar to just cover the fish in a cool oven at 300°F (150°C), gas mark 2 for about 2½ hours. The pieces of eel should be packed together in a shallow dish, and they are cooked when you can pierce them with a small, sharp knife. After cooking, they should be left to cool and jell before eating them with brown bread and butter. Hot eels with mashed potato are another London delicacy.

Earlier in our history we were more adventurous with eels. Mrs Rundell has a recipe for collared eel, cooked whole in a circle and pickled when cold, while Eliza Acton cooks eels in cream. Izaak Walton spit-

roasted his eels, and conger eel soup can still be found in the Channel Islands. Of the eel recipes this pie is my favourite, although I have updated the original, very old recipe.

Eel pie   *serves 4–6*

1 clove of garlic
1 lb (450 g/1 lb) eel
Ground mace
Salt and pepper
A pinch of saffron stamens
2 tbsp (30 ml/2 tbsp) boiling water
2 large cooking apples
Vinegar
4 oz (100 g/1 cup) plain flour (all purpose flour)
1 oz (25 g/2 tbsp) butter
1 oz (25 g/2 tbsp) lard

Skin the garlic clove and cut it in half, rubbing the cut halves around a 1 pt (600 ml/1¼ pt) oval pie dish. Cut the eel into small pieces and sprinkle each piece with a little ground mace mixed with salt and pepper. Put the pieces in the dish. Steep the saffron in the boiling water for 10 minutes. Peel, core and chop the apples into small pieces then simmer them in 2 tbsp (30 ml/2½ tbsp) water until they are soft enough to mash to a purée. Strain the saffron liquid and pour it over the eel pieces, then spoon on the apple purée, filling any gaps with it. Add enough vinegar to barely cover the fish, cover the dish with a piece of buttered foil and bake it in a cool oven at 300°F (150°C), gas mark 2 for about 2 hours or until the fish is tender when pierced with a small, sharp knife.

Allow the dish to cool completely, making the shortcrust pastry in the meantime. Sift the flour with a good pinch of salt into a bowl. Cut the fats into small pieces and rub them into the flour, then mix to a stiff dough with cold water. Knead the pastry lightly and quickly until it is smooth, wrap it in a piece of greaseproof paper and chill it in the refrigerator until the eel dish is completely cold.

Roll the pastry on a lightly floured board until it is at least 1 in (2.5 cm) larger than the pie dish. Cut off a ½ in (1.25 cm) strip all round the pastry. Grease the rim of the dish and stick the strip of pastry in place, cutting and joining it neatly. Moisten it with cold water, cover with the large piece of pastry, pressing the edges to seal them, then trim and decorate them. Any small pieces of pastry can be used to make leaves and tassels to decorate the top of the pie. Brush it with milk or a little beaten egg and bake the pie in a moderately hot oven at 400°F (200°C), gas mark 6 for about 30 minutes or until the pastry is golden brown and cooked.

The pie may be served hot, or cold, when the filling will have jelled.

Kedgeree   *serves 4*

The British brought the recipe back from India, adapting the native dish containing lentils and onions and spices as well as rice and eggs with the addition of smoked fish. Once the foreign ingredients were reduced or eliminated completely, the British accepted kedgeree as one of their traditional breakfast dishes.

8 oz (225 g/generous 1 cup) long grain rice
Salt and pepper
1 lb (450 g/1 lb) smoked haddock
4 oz (100 g/½ cup) butter
2 large hard-boiled eggs
1 level tsp (5 ml/1 level tsp) finely chopped parsley

Sprinkle the rice into a large pan of fast-boiling salted water, stir it then leave it to cook for 12 minutes or until it is just tender. Put the haddock in a pan, just cover it with cold water and simmer it for 10 minutes; it should not boil. When the flesh flakes easily, drain it and flake it, removing skin and bones. Drain the rice well.

  Melt the butter in a large pan and add the rice and stir it well, to coat it with butter. Add the fish pieces and season the mixture with salt and pepper. Cut a few slices from the hard-boiled eggs for garnish, roughly chop the remainder and stir it gently through the rice and fish and when it is thoroughly hot, turn it on to a serving dish and garnish it with the egg slices and parsley.

Mackerel with gooseberry sauce   *serves 4*

4 medium mackerel
Salt and pepper
1 tbsp (15 ml/1 tbsp) cooking oil
12 oz (350 g/12 oz) gooseberries
2 oz (50 g/¼ cup) granulated sugar
1 level dessertspoon (10 ml/1 good dessertspoon) arrowroot (cornstarch)
1 large lemon

Rinse the mackerel under running cold water, pat them dry with kitchen paper and season them inside and out with salt and pepper. Brush half the oil over the sides to be cooked first and arrange them on the grid of the grill pan. Grill for 7 or 8 minutes on each side, brushing with the remaining oil when you turn the mackerel over. Top and tail the gooseberries and put them in a pan with ¼ pt (125 ml/⅔ cup) cold water and the sugar. Simmer the gooseberries gently until they are soft but not disintegrating. Blend the arrowroot (cornstarch) with a little cold water, pour in some of the hot gooseberry liquid, stir well and return this mixture to the pan.

Bring slowly to the boil, stirring all the time until the sauce has thickened.

Finely grate the rind from the lemon and squeeze out and strain the juice. Stir the rind and the juice into the sauce. Check the flavour of the sauce, but resist adding more sugar, otherwise it will be too sweet to accompany the fish. Serve with the grilled mackerel.

Sole cooked in cider   *serves 4*

2 lb (1 kg/2 lb) sole, filleted
½ pt (250 ml/1¼ cups) dry cider
1 oz (25 g/2 tbsp) butter
1 oz (25 g/4 tbsp) plain flour (all purpose flour)
1 tbsp (15 ml/1 tbsp) strained lemon juice
1 level tbsp (15 ml/1 level tbsp) chopped parsley
4 tbsp (60 ml/5 tbsp) single cream (light cream)
Salt and pepper

Skin the fillets removing both the dark and white skin if you wish, then fold each fillet in three with the white skin inside if you have not removed it. Arrange the fish in a buttered shallow dish, pour in the cider and cold water if necessary to just cover the fish. Cover the dish with buttered foil and cook the fish in a moderate oven at 350°F (180°C), gas mark 4 for 15 to 20 minutes.

While the fish cooks, make the sauce. Melt the butter in a pan and stir in the flour. Cook the roux gently for 1 minute until it is sandy-textured then remove the pan from the heat until the fish is ready. Remove the fish from the oven, lift out the fillets, draining them well. Arrange them on a hot serving dish and keep them hot. Strain the fish liquid, then gradually stir ½ pt (250 ml/1¼ cups) of it into the roux to make a smooth liquid. Return the pan to the heat and bring it slowly to the boil, stirring it all the time that the sauce is thickening. Cook the sauce gently for 2 or 3 minutes. Stir in the lemon juice, parsley and cream and season well with salt and pepper. Reheat gently but do not boil the sauce, then pour it over the fish.

Bloater paste   *serves 10*

Herring, left whole and ungutted, are lightly salted and smoked and then re-named bloaters. They should be grilled or fried and eaten on the day they are bought because the mild cure will not preserve them for more than a few days. Those from Yarmouth where the bloater originated are thought to have the finest flavour and the idea of making them into a paste also originated in Yarmouth. There are many variations of the recipe; some versions add spices, one includes hard-boiled eggs, but all agree that the bloater should be pounded with about half its weight in butter to make a rich, smoothly spreading paste. Buckling can be used instead of bloaters, noting that they should be stripped of their skins and bones, seasoned and finished without further cooking.

8 bloaters
1 tbsp (15 ml/1 tbsp) lemon juice
8 oz (225 g/1 cup) unsalted butter—approximately
Freshly ground white pepper
3–4 oz (75–100 g/½ cup) clarified butter

Put the bloaters in a pan, cover them with boiling water and simmer for a few minutes. Drain, removing heads, tails and all bones, then weigh the remaining flesh. Allow half this weight in butter. Finely mince the bloaters twice, adding the lemon juice, then pound the fish in a mortar with the butter to form a smooth paste. Season with white pepper. Turn the mixture into small pots, smooth the surface of each and cover with a thick layer of clarified butter. Leave to set in the refrigerator before serving with fingers of toast as a first course, or spread on bread or toast for tea. A food processor will make short work of the mincing, pounding and blending.

Jugged kippers   *serves 4*

Fat, oily kippers are marvellous; the red-dyed fish in packets are not. Fresh kippers can be fried or grilled, both methods drying them slightly. I prefer this moister method.

4 small kippers   *1 large lemon*
Boiling water   *Mustard or horseradish sauce*

You need a large jug for this, and small kippers, unless you do not mind using a Victorian jug originally made for the wash stand. Put the kippers in the jug, heads down and pour in freshly boiling water right up to their tails. Cover the jug with a saucer and leave the kippers in a warm place for 5 minutes. Then drain them and lift each one out carefully on to a serving plate. Add 2 or 3 lemon slices or wedges and serve with mustard or horseradish sauce.

Grilled herring with mustard sauce   *serves 4*

Should you be unable to buy herring, use sprats instead, still under-rated and therefore inexpensive compared with more popular fish.

4 medium herring or 2 lb (1 kg/2 lb) sprats
Salt and pepper
1 oz (25 g/2 tbsp) butter
1 oz (25 g/4 tbsp) plain flour (all purpose flour)
¾ pt (375 ml/scant 2 cups) fish stock or milk
Ready-mixed English mustard

Scale the herring and rinse them under running cold water then pat each one dry with kitchen paper. Sprats require rinsing inside and out, draining well, then drying on kitchen paper. Line the grill pan with foil before arranging the fish on the grid. Slash each herring on each side, cutting through to the bone at the point where the flesh is thickest then sprinkle herring or sprats with a little salt before grilling them. Because the cooking takes such a short time, make the sauce before you cook the fish.

Melt the butter in a pan and stir in the flour then cook the roux gently for 1 minute. Remove the pan from the heat and gradually stir in the fish stock, which is preferable, or milk. Bring the sauce to the boil, stirring all the time, then lower the heat and simmer it for about 5 minutes, stirring it occasionally. Now grill the fish quickly until they are golden and crisp on each side. Stir some ready-made English mustard into the sauce, adding 1 level tsp (5 ml/1 level tsp) to start and tasting the sauce before adding more. Then add salt and pepper.

If you prefer the milder flavour of French mustard, use this instead of English mustard.

Soused herring   *serves 4*

Herring were the mainstay of the British fishing industry until quite recently when over-fishing has made catches scarce and the price high. Traditional fishing ports for herring catches such as Yarmouth, Peel in the Isle of Man, Seahouses in Northumberland and the Loch Fyne coast of western Scotland turned part of the catch into kippers, by splitting the herring complete with its head, gutting it and smoking it, or bloaters, which are left whole and ungutted and slightly salted before they are smoked. Fresh herring, once soused, can also be kept for a few days, like kippers and bloaters, but unlike these, soused herring can be served for a light summer lunch. If you cannot buy herring, this recipe works for mackerel.

4 medium herring
¼ pt (125 ml/⅔ cup) white wine vinegar
Salt
4 small bay leaves
4 sprigs of thyme
Black peppercorns
4 blades of mace
1 small onion
Watercress or parsley to garnish

Scrape the scales off the herring then cut off their heads. Remove the backbones. Clean the fish inside and out under running cold water, re-serving any roe. Pat the herring dry, replace the roes inside the fish and either lay the fish in a shallow earthenware dish, nose to tail, or flatten each one on a board and roll from the head end to the tail with the roes inside. Secure rolled herring with wooden cocktail sticks then arrange them in the dish letting the tails stick up. Pour on the white wine vinegar and an equal quantity of water to cover the fish, except for the tails, sprinkle them with a little salt and add the bay leaves, thyme, a couple of dozen peppercorns and the mace. Skin and finely slice the onion, separate each slice into rings and strew the rings over the fish. Cover the dish with foil, tucking it under the rim to confine the fishy smell during cooking and bake the herring in a moderate oven 350°F (180°C), gas mark 4 for 30 minutes then allow them to cool in the liquid. If it is more convenient, the fish may be cooked more slowly in a cooler oven 300°F (150°C), gas mark 2 for 1 to 1½ hours.

To serve the herring, lift them from the vinegar, allow them to drain, then garnish them with watercress or parsley.

Meat and Game

For a long time we have accepted good meat as part of our lives, so it might not have occurred to you that meat is becoming as tasteless as modern chickens. Pigs are intensively reared, and sheep and cattle, while spending much of their time in pastures, have their feed supplemented with concentrates guaranteed to produce market weight animals in a few days, thus saving money but losing flavour and quality.

Game is rarely seen, the chain butchers' shops do not handle it and one has to look for the old sign, Butcher, Poulterer and Game Dealer, to have any hope at all of walking in and buying over the counter. Pigeons are dirty birds, rabbits we regard with suspicion. Aren't they all diseased? Memories die hard. And wood pigeons are very different from the birds which inhabit our buildings, damaging the stonework. Hares are as scarce as game birds, except for pheasant and grouse, again reared almost on a factory-farming level by gamekeepers.

Nowadays we will not handle heads and tails, feet and innards, and even prepared offal dishes are not favoured. No cook would serve boiled sheep's head with brain sauce, pig's trotters or a liver dish for a dinner party without having invited guests of a similar persuasion. Otherwise, imagine the number of omelettes she would have to cook.

It is ten years since I cooked a pig's head, something I would have done again sooner, and regularly, if they were in the butchers' shops to remind me. From my butcher, I buy spring lamb, brought from the Welsh hills early in May. It is a standing order, although I do not know when I will buy my first pieces. It is one of those marvellous seasonal surprises, all too few these days.

Roast beef, lamb or pork

Plain roast meat has long been a strongpoint of English cookery, in times past on a spit in front of an open fire, latterly in wood-burning stoves superseded by the modern cooker. With improved methods of rearing cattle, sheep and pigs, flavour improved and meat became leaner. The finest piece of lamb I have ever eaten was in Cumbria, a roast leg of Swaledale lamb which had spent its life on top of the heathery hills. As I write, British Meat are about to release the results of a two-year study of roasting meat methods, which, I am told, need give us little cause for alarm because we have been doing the right things with our meat through the trials and errors of cooks long gone.

Beef

The best roasting cuts of beef are sirloin, forerib, fillet, aitchbone, middlerib, wingrib and topside. The three former are the prime cuts suitable for roasting in a hot oven at 425°F (220°C), gas mark 7 for 15 minutes to each 1 lb (450 g/1 lb) plus 15 minutes extra for rare meat. Allow 20 minutes per 1 lb (450 g/1 lb) plus an extra 20 minutes for medium and 25 minutes for well done. The aitchbone, middlerib, wingrib and topside cuts should be roasted in a moderately hot oven 375°F (190°C), gas mark 5 for 25 minutes per 1 lb (450 g/1 lb) for joints on the bone and thin pieces of meat. Allow 30 minutes to each 1 lb (450 g/1 lb) for thick pieces or boned and rolled meats.

Cover all meat to be roasted generously with beef dripping and baste it frequently during the roasting time.

Serve with Yorkshire pudding, see page 29, horseradish sauce, page 87 and roast potatoes. Include a green vegetable and good gravy too.

Lamb

Although you can roast just about any cut of lamb, the best ones are leg, shoulder, loin, best end, breast and the saddle which is the loin cut from either side of the animal left as one piece. It is a large joint, very much a celebration cut. We are gradually accepting the idea from France that lamb is delicious served pink rather than cooked in the British fashion, very well done. Roast the lamb in a moderately hot oven at 375°F (190°C), gas mark 5 for 25 minutes to each 1 lb (450 g/1 lb) for leg, best end, loin and saddle joints. Shoulder and breast of lamb is best cooked in a moderate oven at 325°F (160°C), gas mark 3 allowing about 40 minutes per 1 lb (450 g/1 lb), particularly if you bone, roll and stuff these cuts.

Lamb has enough fat on it to be roasted without additional fat. Lightly sprinkle the skin with salt, stand the meat on a grid in the roasting tin and do not baste it during cooking. You will then find the meat succulent with a crisp skin.

Serve lamb with mint sauce or jelly or redcurrant jelly. Onion sauce is an old favourite, or if preferred, make a rich onion gravy, see page 84. Serve with potatoes and a green vegetable.

Pork

Roast the leg, hand and spring, belly, loin or tenderloin cuts. Because most of the pig joints are large, they are often divided, and so you might buy the knuckle or fillet end of a leg, the knuckle or blade of a hand and spring or whatever weight you require of the loin. Pork must be well cooked so allow 35 minutes to each 1 lb (450 g/1 lb) plus another 25 minutes in a moderately hot oven at 375°F (190°C) gas mark 5 for thick

joints such as leg, or a part of it, or the whole or part of the hand and spring. Thinner cuts should be cooked at the same temperature but for 30 minutes to each 1 lb (450 g/1 lb) plus another 30 minutes.

Ask your butcher to score the skin and prior to roasting rub the skin with a little oil, sprinkle it lightly with salt and roast it without extra fat. Do not baste the meat during the cooking. This method gives a truly crisp crackling, lightly seasoned and delicious.

Serve pork with apple sauce (leaving it tart rather than adding sweetening), sage and onion stuffing, thick gravy and roast or mashed potatoes and a green vegetable.

Cornish pasties   *makes 6*

Whichever recipe one uses, there are always complaints and from letters I draw the conclusion that it is as right to crimp the pastry on the top as it is to crimp it on the side. The meat should be chopped into small pieces, not minced; it may or may not contain potato, turnip or other root vegetables. Originally these pasties were made in Cornwall as a convenient packed lunch, the pastry enclosing both sweet and savoury fillings divided by a pastry partition. Recently I was told that the original pastry was a tough, hard stuff, not eaten but substantial enough to remain whole even though carried around all day. This makes sense but I wonder how the Cornish workers then ate the filling; presumably with their fingers, so it must have been fairly dry. Nowadays, they are always made from shortcrust pastry, the aim being to produce a crust that is short and meltingly fragile.

12 oz (375 g/3 cups) plain flour (all purpose flour)
Salt and pepper
3 oz (75 g/6 tbsp) margarine
3 oz (75 g/6 tbsp) lard   *8 oz (225 g/8 oz) potatoes*
1 lb (450 g/1 lb) skirt or chuck steak   2 oz (50 g/2 oz) turnip
1 small onion   *1 small egg, size 4 or 5*

Sift the flour and a good pinch of salt into a bowl. Rub in the margarine and lard and mix to a stiff dough with cold water. Knead the pastry lightly until smooth then wrap it and chill it in the refrigerator while you prepare the filling.

Cut the lean meat into small pieces, smaller than you would for a casserole or stew, and discard any skin, gristle and fat. Skin and finely chop the onion. Peel the potatoes and turnip piece. Slice half the potato and dice the remaining vegetables. Mix the vegetables with the meat and season them well with salt and pepper. Roll the pastry on a lightly floured board and cut it into 6 rounds using a 6 in (15 cm) plate as a guide. Lay the potato slices on the pastry (this layer ensures the pasties stay a good shape) then put the meat mixture on top. Add 1 tsp (5 ml/1 tsp) water to each filling. Moisten the edge of the pastry rounds and gather the two sides of the pastry to meet over the top of the filling, pressing the edges to seal them and crimping them between finger and thumb. With a skewer make a small hole in the crimped pastry, pushing it between the two pieces, through the join and into the meat. Lightly beat the egg and use to brush the pasties, standing them on a lightly greased baking sheet.

Bake them in a moderately hot oven at 400°F (200°C), gas mark 6 for 20 minutes or until the pastry is set and only just beginning to colour, then lower the temperature to moderate, 350°F (180°C), gas mark 4 and continue cooking for another 40 or 50 minutes. You can check whether the meat is tender by pushing the skewer through the hole you made. If the filling is still resistant to the skewer's probing, cook the pasties longer, covering them with greaseproof paper if the pastry is already brown enough. Serve them hot or cold.

Mulligatawny soup   *serves 4–6*

This is a lightly curried soup which became popular throughout England during the time of the British in India. For recipes, one has to look back to Mrs Beeton; rarely is it featured in cookery books written after the turn of the century.

3 large onions
1 clove of garlic
2 oz (50 g/¼ cup) dripping
2 level tbsp (30 ml/2 good tbsp) curry powder
4 rashers unsalted back bacon
1¾ pt (1 l/4½ cups) chicken stock
2 chicken joints

Skin and finely slice the onions and skin and crush the clove of garlic. Heat the dripping in a large saucepan and fry the onions and garlic very gently for about 10 minutes until soft and turning golden brown. Stir in the curry powder and cook it gently for 1 minute. Remove the rinds from the bacon and chop the rashers into small pieces. Add them to the pan with the stock and chicken joints and bring the soup to the boil. Reduce the heat, cover the pan and simmer the soup for 1 hour or until the chicken joints are cooked. Lift out the chicken joints and when cool enough to handle, remove the meat from the bones in good sized pieces and return them to the pan. Check the seasoning, adding salt and pepper if necessary and serve hot.

Mrs Beeton's recipe includes 1 oz (25 g/2 tbsp) ground almonds pounded to a paste with a little of the stock and added at the last moment before serving. She also adds some mango juice, but because mangoes are not readily available all year round, I use finely chopped mango chutney or pickle as well as the almonds.

Steak and kidney pudding   *serves 6–8*

The tendency nowadays where meats and pastry are combined is to cook the meat first then add a crust and cook for 30 minutes or so. While I think this method is less good with shortcrust and puff pastry pies, it is certainly an improvement with steamed puddings, reducing the cooking time by 2 or 3 hours, a considerable saving in fuel, and allowing the suet crust pastry to remain soft but not sodden. It is essential, however, that the cooked meat be completely cold before it is put into the pastry-lined basin, therefore it is worth cooking it the day before you are to serve it.

2 lb (1 kg/2 lb) chuck or skirt steak
8 oz (225 g/8 oz) ox kidney
1 oz (25 g/4 tbsp) plain flour (all purpose flour)
Salt and pepper
1 large onion
2 oz (50 g/4 tbsp) good beef dripping
1 pt (600 ml/2½ cups) beef stock including a little red wine
8 oz (225 g/8 oz) large mushrooms
A few parsley stalks

3 sprigs of thyme
1 bay leaf
1 blade of mace
10 oz (300 g/2¼ cups) self-raising flour (all purpose flour with raising agent)
1 level tsp (5 ml/1 level tsp) baking powder
5 oz (125 g/1 generous cup) chopped suet

Cut the steak into 1 in (2.5 cm) pieces, discarding gristle, but leaving a little of the fat on the meat for flavour. Cut the kidney into slightly smaller pieces, removing the core, fat and any skin. Mix the plain flour (all purpose flour) with plenty of salt and pepper and use to coat the meats, shaking off the excess. Skin and roughly chop the onion. Heat the dripping in a large pan and fry the onion gently for about 8 minutes until it is soft and just beginning to colour, then remove it from the pan, draining off as much fat as possible. Fry the meats in batches, stirring them so that they brown evenly on all sides, transferring the pieces as they brown either to a casserole for cooking in the oven or on to a plate if you wish to return them to the saucepan for cooking on top of the stove. Sprinkle any remaining seasoned flour into the pan, pour in the stock with some red wine. Even 1 tbsp (15 ml/1 tbsp) wine will improve the flavour. Bring the mixture to the boil and boil it hard, stirring all the time, then either pour it over the meat and onions in the casserole or return the meat and onions to the stock in the saucepan.

Trim the mushroom stalks, separating them from the caps and if they are large slice them with the caps. Add them to the meat. Tie the parsley stalks, thyme sprigs, bay leaf and blade of mace in a neat bundle with a piece of string or enclose them in a small square of muslin and add this bouquet garni to the pan. Cover with a lid and simmer on top of the stove for 1½ to 2 hours or in a slow oven 300°F (150°C), gas mark 2 for the same length of time, or until the meat is almost tender. Cool the meat completely, preferably overnight.

Sift the self-raising flour (all purpose flour with raising agent) with a pinch of salt and the baking powder, then mix in the suet. It is worth the trouble of buying a piece of suet from the butcher and either chopping it finely or grating it coarsely, removing the skin at the same time. The flavour is finer and you will not have the extra flour used to coat shredded suet altering your pastry proportions. Use a little cold water to mix to a soft but not sticky dough. Roll the dough on a lightly floured board (use as little flour as possible) having set aside a quarter of the dough for the lid. Fold the dough into a half-circle and with your hands form the half-circle almost to a quarter-circle, more of a jelly bag shape really. The top edge will wrinkle but this does not matter, because now you roll the point of the bag to extend it slightly, so forming a basin lining without any joins. Flour your fist, put it in the bag and lift it into a lightly greased 3 pt

($1\frac{1}{2}$ l/3–4 pt) pudding basin and smooth the pastry flat against the sides. Fill the basin to within 1 in (2.5 cm) of the top edge, pouring off at least half of the stock to serve as gravy. Roll the reserved pastry into a round for the lid, moisten the edge of the pastry in the basin and cover the pudding, pinching the two edges together all round to make a good seal. Cover the pudding with foil, either pleating it under the rim of the basin or securing it with string, but leaving it fairly loose so that the pudding has room to rise. Fold a long strip of foil, stand the basin on it and use to lift the basin in and out of the steamer. If you need to replenish the water in the bottom pan during the cooking, top it up with boiling water, and make sure that as little steam as possible escapes during the cooking. If you wish to boil the pudding, lower it into gently boiling water which should come no higher than two-thirds of the way up the sides of the basin. Keep the water steadily bubbling throughout and cook the pudding for 2 hours, longer will not harm it, although a shorter cooking time may not be sufficient to make the meat tender.

When cooked, remove the coverings, clean up the basin if necessary, wrap it in a white napkin and send it to the table to be served straight from the basin. Potatoes need not be served; they will certainly provide a substantial accompaniment but the colour is similar to the suet crust pastry. If you need a root vegetable, serve turnips, swedes, parsnips or carrots, but do include sprouts or another green vegetable.

Boiled beef and carrots with dumplings   *serves 4–6*

When a dish becomes lauded in poem or song you can be sure it is good. So it is with boiled beef and carrots; although enjoyed all over the country, it took the London Cockney to sing its praises in an old music hall song. Salted silverside is the traditional cut to use, but salt brisket or topside will do. What seems to be a fairly cheap dish is in reality quite expensive because only the larger pieces of meat will cook to succulence, but they certainly have more flavour.

4 lb (2 kg/4 lb) salted silverside or an even larger piece
6 medium onions
12 cloves
2 lb (1 kg/2 lb) carrots
2 blades of mace
A small handful of black peppercorns
4 oz (100 g/1 cup) self-raising flour (all purpose flour with raising agent)
A pinch of baking powder
A good pinch of salt   2 oz (50 g/4 tbsp) finely chopped suet

The brine which butchers use for salting beef is rarely very salty these days and 7 to 10 days is the maximum period for keeping meat in the brine, so it is not necessary to soak salt beef in cold water after buying it, but it is always wise to check with your own butcher. Put the piece of beef in a large pan, but not so large that it will be swimming in water. The onions may be left unskinned (but washed), the skins improving the colour of the stock, or skinned, cutting off roots and tops, but not too close otherwise the onion disintegrates during cooking. Stick the cloves into the onions and add them to the pan. Peel the carrots, removing roots and tops and add them whole with the mace and peppercorns. Add water to barely cover the meat, bring it to simmering point, cover the pan, and leave the meat for 3½ to 4 hours or until it is very tender.

Before you cover the pan and leave the meat simmering, remove any scum that has formed and if the water is very salty after 10 or 15 minutes simmering, pour it away and begin again with fresh water.

Sift the flour for the dumplings with the extra baking powder and a good pinch of salt. Stir in the chopped suet and mix to a soft but not sticky dough with cold water. Form the dough into small balls by rolling pieces between floured hands. When the meat is cooked, remove it from the stock on to a hot plate and scoop out and drain the carrots, arranging them around the meat. Keep the meat warm, while you reheat the stock, then add the dumplings and simmer them, covered, for 10 to 15 minutes, depending on the size, until they are much enlarged and fluffy-looking.

In the meantime, slice the beef after it has stood and settled for about 10 minutes, and serve it with carrots and dumplings. The gravy should be some of the stock from the pan, not thickened, but if it is lacking in flavour, remove a good jugful from the pan before adding the dumplings and boil it hard in a pan to reduce it and concentrate the flavour. Serve it in a small jug.

When cold, boiled beef makes excellent sandwiches, or if you prefer it warm, return it to the pan and bring it slowly to simmering point, so that it heats through to the centre, before slicing it and making sandwiches. Do not use the beef on its own; it is always nicer spread with a little mustard or horseradish sauce.

Shepherd's pie   *serves 6–8*

Sometimes called cottage pie. Best when made with cold roast beef which is the traditional ingredient; now sadly too expensive.

1 large onion
2 oz (50 g/4 tbsp) good beef dripping
1 lb (450 g/1 lb) skirt or chuck steak, or shin of beef
14 oz (397 g/14 oz) can tomatoes
Salt and pepper
1 level tbsp (15 ml/1 level tbsp) cornflour (cornstarch)

1 level tsp (5 ml/1 level tsp) finely chopped fresh thyme
2 lb (1 kg/2 lb) potatoes
3 oz (75 g/6 tbsp) butter
4 tbsp (60 ml/5 tbsp) milk
2 oz (50 g/¼ cup) grated Cheddar cheese

Skin and finely chop the onion and fry it for about 8 minutes in the dripping. Meanwhile, finely chop or mince the meat, cutting away skin, fat and gristly bits. Add the meat to the pan, stir it round for 4 or 5 minutes until it has browned, then add the tomatoes, breaking them down with a fork. Add some of the tomato liquid if necessary. Bring to the boil, then lower the heat and let the mixture simmer for 15 minutes. Season well with salt and plenty of pepper then blend the cornflour (cornstarch) with a little water, stir it in with the thyme and continue cooking.

Meanwhile, peel the potatoes, cut them into even-sized pieces and cook them in boiling salted water. Drain well, dry them if necessary and mash them with the butter and milk and plenty of salt and pepper. Turn the mince into an oval pie dish and cover it with mashed potato, forking it into a pattern. Sprinkle with the cheese and bake the pie in a moderately hot oven at 400°F (200°C), gas mark 6 for 15 minutes, then reduce the heat to moderate, 350°F (180°C), gas mark 4 and continue to cook it for 40 to 50 minutes more.

Lamb hot-pot   *serves 4–6*

Stews or casseroles of lamb (originally mutton) belong firmly to regional cookery. Lancashire hot-pot is the English version of Irish stew; there's lobscouse from Liverpool and a version from Scotland similar to the Lancashire recipe. But as well as these distinctive variations, there are any number of recipes using lamb as a basis, each one differing slightly by the use of stock, cider or ale, this or that vegetable, some or no herbs. Pearl barley is all I insist on in a lamb stew.

2 lb (1 kg/2 lb) scrag neck of lamb
½ oz (15 g/2 tbsp) plain flour (all purpose flour)
Salt and pepper
1 oz (25 g/2 tbsp) dripping
8 oz (225 g/8 oz) onions　　　　*A few parsley stalks*
3 oz (75 g/6 tbsp) pearl barley　　*3 sprigs of thyme*
Good stock　　　　　　　　　　*1 blade of mace*

Scrag neck is a fatty meat full of bones, but also full of flavour. If you prefer something less fiddly to eat, use stewing lamb or cutlets. Season the flour with plenty of salt and pepper and use to coat the meat. Heat the dripping in a pan and brown the pieces of meat on both sides, transferring them as they brown to a deep casserole with a lid. Skin and roughly chop the onions and fry them in the remaining fat for 8 minutes until they soften and begin to colour, then transfer them to the casserole. Add the rinsed pearl barley and enough stock to barely cover the meat. Tie the parsley stalks, thyme sprigs and blade of mace in a bundle with a piece of string or tie them in a small piece of muslin. Add them to the casserole with more salt and pepper. Cover the casserole and cook it in a moderate oven at 325°F (160°C), gas mark 3 for 2 hours or for a similar time in a saucepan on top of the stove.

The barley will thicken the stock of this simple, but good dish.

Pork pie   *serves 4–6*

There is no alternative to hot water crust paste for the traditional pork pie with its jellied stock filling the holes left as the meat shrinks in cooking. But for drier mixtures such as pieces of chicken mixed with sausagemeat, a shortcrust pastry will do and it can be moulded in a cake tin to look like a raised pie.

1 veal knuckle or 2 pig's trotters
Pork bones
1 medium onion
3 cloves
A small handful of black peppercorns
A few parsley stalks
1 blade of mace
4 sprigs of thyme
Salt and pepper
2 lb (1 kg/2 lb) pork shoulder meat with some fat
8 oz (225 g/8 oz) unsmoked back bacon rashers
1 level tsp (5 ml/1 level tsp) finely chopped fresh sage
½ level tsp (2.5 ml/½ level tsp) ground nutmeg
½ level tsp (2.5 ml/½ level tsp) ground mace
½ level tsp (2.5 ml/½ level tsp) ground allspice
4 oz (100 g/½ cup) lard
1 lb (450 g/1 lb) plain flour (all purpose flour)
1 small egg, size 4

Rinse the veal knuckle or the pig's trotters which should be split by the butcher and the pork bones and put them in a large pan; cover with cold water. Skin the onion, stick it with the cloves and add it to the pan. Add the peppercorns, parsley stalks, blade of mace and sprigs of thyme. Cover the pan and simmer the contents steadily for 4 hours, then strain the stock into a clean pan and boil it hard until it is reduced to approximately ¾ pt (400 ml/scant 2 cups). Check the seasoning of the stock, adding salt and pepper to taste.

While the stock reduces, cut the pork into small pieces. You should have one part of fat to about four parts of lean meat for this recipe. Remove the bacon rinds and very finely chop or mince the rashers. Mix the meat with the bacon, fresh sage, salt and pepper, nutmeg, mace and allspice.

For the hot water crust paste, boil the lard with 7 fl oz (195 ml/scant 1 cup) water. Sift the flour with ½ level tsp (2.5 ml/½ level tsp) salt into a bowl and as soon as the lard mixture boils, pour it at once into the flour and mix to a dough with a wooden spoon. As soon as the dough can be handled comfortably (but do not let it cool completely), remove a quarter of it for the lid and put the rest into a 6 in (15 cm) loose-bottomed cake tin. Quickly mould the dough up the sides of the tin, smoothing it on the base and making sure it is free of cracks.

Pack the pork filling into the pie, then roll the reserved piece of dough into a circle for the lid and stick it in place with a little beaten egg. Neaten the edge by cutting round with scissors and make a fairly large hole in the centre, decorating it with leaves and tassels formed from any remaining dough. It is essential to keep reserved dough warm; when it becomes cold it is unworkable. Keep the central hole open during the cooking with a small tube of foil.

Brush the pie with beaten egg and bake it in a moderately hot oven at 400°F (200°C), gas mark 6 for about 30 minutes until the pastry firms, then lower the temperature to moderate 350°F (180°C), gas mark 4 and continue cooking for another 2 hours. If you have any beaten egg left, brush the pie again when you lower the oven. Cover the top of the pie towards the end of the cooking time if it begins to darken too much.

Finally remove the pie from the cake tin, brush the sides with beaten egg and return the pie to the oven for 10 minutes or so until the sides turn a good shiny golden brown.

Heat the jellied stock until it is liquid and pour some of it into the pie through the central hole using a small funnel or one fashioned from two or three thicknesses of foil. Allow to cool all day or overnight before cutting.

Faggots   *serves 6*

Faggots were the perfect way of using up the bits and pieces left after a pig was killed and often included lights and melts. Butchers who make their own faggots usually include them, rather than using cuts which could be sold over the counter. Recipes vary enormously around the country and they are often jokingly called savoury ducks or poor man's goose. If you make them, use the bits and pieces you can happily handle, but do not do without the caul fat which encloses each faggot, keeping it moist during cooking. Caul fat is not easy to find, you will have to try the smaller butcher's shop of the older more traditional kind.

*2 lb (1 kg/2 lb) pig's bits and pieces to include liver, heart, melt, lights, or
    belly pork*
1 lb (450 g/1 lb) caul fat
12 oz (375 g/12 oz) onions
2 large cloves of garlic
3 sage leaves or a good pinch of dried sage
4 oz (100 g/1¼ cups) breadcrumbs
2 large eggs, size 2
Salt and pepper
1 level tsp (5 ml/1 level tsp) ground nutmeg
¼ pt (125 ml/⅔ cup) good stock

Mince the chosen meats, discarding gristle and other pieces which will
not go through the mincer. Put the caul fat into a large bowl, cover it with
warm water and leave it to soften. Skin and finely chop the onions and the
garlic cloves. Finely chop fresh sage leaves. Mix the onions and garlic with
the meat, adding fresh or dried sage, and turn the mixture into a frying
pan or saucepan. Cook it very gently for about 30 minutes, stirring occasionally. It should be cooked on a very low heat so that the juices run out
of the meat and the mixture cooks lightly without browning. Strain off
the juices and reserve them. Mix the meat with the breadcrumbs, beaten
eggs, salt and pepper and the nutmeg to make a firm mixture that is easy
to handle, adding the breadcrumbs and egg with care as the mixture
begins to bind. Drain the caul fat, spread it on a work surface and cut it
into 5 in (13 cm) squares. Divide the meat mixture between the squares,
shaping each piece into a ball and wrapping the fat around it. Arrange the
faggots in a shallow dish, with the caul fat gathers underneath and side by
side, close together. Pour in the stock (not the reserved juices) and bake
the faggots in a moderate oven 350°F (180°C), gas mark 4 for 40 minutes to
1 hour or until the tops of the faggots are well browned.

While they cook, stand the reserved juices on ice cubes to cool them
quickly, so that the fat rises to the top and can be removed easily. Pour the
remaining stock over the faggots about 10 minutes before the end of the
cooking time.

Traditionally, faggots are served with a purée of dried peas; see pease
pudding on page 46.

Oxford sausages   *makes 25*

Minced or finely chopped mixtures of meats such as offal and off-cuts left
after butchery were made into sausages and every maker had his or her
individual recipe. These sausages combine veal with pork, the mixture
shaped by hand rather than by being stuffed into skins.

1 lb (450 g/1 lb) lean pork
1 lb (450 g/1 lb) veal

1 lb (450 g/1 lb) beef suet
8 oz (225 g/3 cups) fresh white breadcrumbs
Salt and pepper
A pinch of dried marjoram
A pinch of dried thyme
A good pinch of dried sage
1 tsp (5 ml/1 tsp) ground nutmeg
Grated rind of ½ lemon
2 egg yolks

Mince or finely chop the pork and veal. Use a block of suet rather than the ready-shredded kind and grate it, removing all the fine skin. Mix with the meats, using your hands, adding the breadcrumbs, salt and pepper, marjoram, thyme, sage, nutmeg and lemon rind and bind the mixture with the egg yolks, mixing well. Form into sausage shapes, lightly flouring your hands each time, or form the mixture into flat patties. Fry gently at first in a heavy frying pan and when the fat begins to run increase the heat and continue to fry the sausages for about 30 minutes, turning them frequently.

Roast game

Only young game should be roasted. Older birds and animals should be casseroled. If you are in any doubt at all about the age of the game, err on the safe side and treat it to long slow, moist cooking. All game must be hung before it is plucked or eviscerated, otherwise it will be tough and lack flavour. Times vary from 2 to 3 days for wild duck and young grouse, 3 to 5 days for partridge and about 7 days for pheasant. Humid weather will rapidly increase the rate at which game becomes ready for cooking; if you are hanging game in such weather, keep a close watch on it, cooking it or, at least, preparing it for the freezer when it is ready, which may well be sooner than you expect. Cold weather, on the other hand, slows down the rate at which game matures in flavour and 10 days may be needed for pheasant and joints of venison. Hang all birds by their necks, rabbits, hares and venison by the hind legs, and separately so that the air can circulate. If you wish to collect the blood of rabbits and hares for thickening the sauce, tie a small plastic bag over each muzzle.

Plucking game is a pest of a job, slow and sneezy work. Hold the bird inside a large plastic bag, the stouter the bag the better, and pull out the feathers in the direction of growth so that the skin does not tear. A really damp cloth or a bowl of water is essential for removing feathers which stick to your fingers. Wing tips, heads, feet and other unwanted bits should be cut off before you remove the innards through a small cut in the vent. Ease the entrails away from the rib cage with curved fingers. You will feel them come loose and you can hook them out in one parcel, linked by membranes. Reserve the heart, liver and gizzard for gravy, if it is to be made, cutting bile stains off the liver and slitting the gizzard so you can pull away the wrinkled lining complete with the bird's last dinner of grain. Rinse well and cook with flavourings to make stock.

Most game will require fat on the breast during roasting—softened butter, pork fat or strips of unsmoked fat bacon.

The following chart comes from The Game Conservancy, Fordingbridge, Hampshire, and the excellent *Game Cookery Book* compiled for them by Julia Drysdale contains detailed information about all types of game. I recommend it if you are becoming newly acquainted with game straight from the bag.

Game chart

Game	*Weights*	*Servings*	*Temperature and roasting times*
Common snipe	3½–4½ oz (100–130 g)	1 or 2 per person	450°F (230°C), gas mark 8 for 6–15 minutes
Capercaillie	6–12 lb (2¾–5½ kg)	5	braise or stew
Geese	6–10 lb (2¾–5 kg)	6	425°F (220°C), gas mark 7 for 10 minutes then 325°F (160°C), gas mark 3 for 1 hour
Grouse	1¼–1½ lb (600–700 g)	1–2	375°F (190°C), gas mark 5 for 35 minutes
Hares	6½–7 lb (3–3¼ kg)	6–10	400°F (200°C), gas mark 6 for 20 minutes per 1 lb (450 g) or 300°F (150°C), gas mark 2 for 1½–2 hours
Mallard	2¼–2¾ lb (1–1⅓ kg)	2–3	450°F (230°C), gas mark 8 for 20–30 minutes
Partridge	13–15 oz (350–450 g)	1–2	425°F (220°C), gas mark 7 for 30 minutes
Pheasant	3–3½ lb (1⅓–1⅔ kg)	4	375°F (190°C), gas mark 5 for ¾–1 hour
Ptarmigan	1–1¼ lb (400–600 g)	1	braise or stew
Rabbits	2¼–3½ lb (1–1⅔ kg)	3–4	400°F (200°C), gas mark 6 for 1 hour
Teal	11–13 oz (300–370 g)	1	425°F (220°C), gas mark 7 for 10–15 minutes
Widgeon	1½–2 lb (700–900 g)	2	425°F (220°C), gas mark 7 for 15–25 minutes
Woodcock	8–14 oz (230–400 g)	1	425°F (220°C), gas mark 7 for 15–20 minutes
Wood pigeon	1–1¼ lb (500–600 g)	1	425°F (220°C), gas mark 7 for 20 minutes

Game casserole   *serves 6*

This is a useful recipe for older birds, those about whose age you are uncertain, and damaged birds.

8 oz (225 g/8 oz) unsmoked streaky bacon rashers
Approximately 3 lb (1½ kg/3 lb) weight of game birds, rabbit, hare or
  venison joints
1 lb (450 g/1 lb) onions
4 sticks of celery
1¾ pt (1 l/scant 4½ cups) game stock or good beef stock
¼ pt (125 ml/⅔ cup) red wine
A few parsley stalks
3 sprigs of thyme
1 blade of mace
1 bay leaf
Salt and pepper
1 oz (25 g/2 tbsp) beef dripping
1 oz (25 g/4 tbsp) plain flour (all purpose flour)
8 oz (225 g/8 oz) button mushrooms
1 level tbsp (15 ml/1 good tbsp) finely chopped fresh parsley

Remove the rinds from the bacon and fry them in a large pan until the fat runs freely. Chop the rashers roughly. Remove the rinds, add the bacon to the pan and fry it gently for 3 or 4 minutes, again until the fat runs freely, then add the game birds or joints of game and brown them on all sides, transferring them to a casserole as they brown. Skin and finely chop the onions and add them to the fat in the pan and cook them gently for 5 to 8 minutes until they are just beginning to colour, adding the chopped celery after 2 or 3 minutes' cooking. Transfer the contents of the pan to the casserole.

Pour in the stock and red wine. Tie the parsley stalks, thyme sprigs, mace and bay leaf in a bundle with string or wrap them in a small piece of muslin secured with cotton or string. Add to the pan with plenty of salt and pepper. Cook the casserole in a moderate oven at 325°F (160°C), gas mark 3) for 2 to 3 hours depending on the type and thickness of the meat, but until it is tender anyway.

While the casserole cooks, melt the dripping in a frying pan, stir in the flour and cook it very slowly on the lowest heat for 10 minutes or until the flour is a good rich brown. Remove some of the stock from the casserole and gradually stir it into the pan and bring the mixture to the boil, stirring all the time it thickens. Reduce the heat and let the sauce simmer for 20 to 30 minutes then rinse the mushrooms, leaving them whole if they are small, otherwise halving them. Add them to the pan and season with salt and pepper. Continue to cook for another 10 to 15 minutes, then check the seasoning and stir in the parsley.

Remove the casserole from the oven, gently stir this sauce into the casserole and serve it, cutting whole birds, if large, in half.

Potted game *serves 4*

A useful recipe for making something delicious from small pieces of cooked game. Bear in mind, too, that this is also good when made with pieces of cooked poultry, beef, lamb or pork or a mixture of meats. And it's a quicker and easier method of using odds and ends than making pâté.

This recipe is deliberately proportioned for small amounts; it's not my experience that one has pounds of cooked meat suddenly available to be used. However, if you wish to produce large quantities of potted meat, then cook a large amount of meat in excess of your needs for the immediate meal.

4 oz (100 g/4 oz) cooked game meat
1 oz (25 g/1 oz) fat cooked bacon
6–9 oz (150–250 g/¾–1¼ cups) unsalted butter
Salt and pepper
Tabasco sauce or Worcester sauce
A little lemon juice or wine

Stewed game is more successful than drier roast game. Dry the former on kitchen paper before preparing it otherwise liquid will collect at the base of your pots; the latter will require a teaspoon or so of stock or wine to moisten it.

Chop the meat coarsely, removing skin, bones and sinewy pieces, aiming for 4 oz (100 g/4 oz) when it is chopped. Melt the butter slowly, allow the solids to fall to the base of the saucepan then let the mixture cool completely. Skim off the clarified butter from the top, using this both for pounding the meat and for covering the pots to finish them. Mix at least a half quantity of butter to meat, pounding the mixture to a paste preferably with a pestle and mortar or with the end of a rolling pin in a stout bowl. For speed use a liquidizer or food processor, stopping the machine before the mixture is reduced to a completely textureless mass. Season the mixture to taste with salt and pepper, Tabasco or Worcester sauce and a little lemon juice or wine. The amount of seasoning will depend very much on whether you use well-seasoned game which has been casseroled in wine or whether you use plainer-cooked meat. Pack the meat mixture into small pots, smoothing the surface and leaving room to float a layer of clarified butter on top which will seal and preserve the meat. Scoop off some more of the top layer of butter from the saucepan, melt it until it is liquid then pour a good layer on top of each pot of meat.

This makes a very tasty first course, or a good sandwich filling.

Pigeon or rook pie   *serves 4–6*

Rooks are rarely used for pies these days, except perhaps in some farm-house kitchens, and in times of plenty, we have forgotten that the pigeon makes a tasty meal. Both rooks and pigeons are cleared in spring in an effort to prevent damage to the farm crops pushing their way through the sun-warmed soil. This recipe works for either bird, although rooks should only be used in the spring when they are the size of small pigeons. Use only the breast meat, discarding the remainder of the rooks. The carcass has a bitter taste and is inedible. If pigeons are in good supply, then use only the breast meat of these birds too, although the remainder of the bird is edible and can be used for stock-making.

4–6 rooks or pigeons
Milk
8 oz (225 g/8 oz) stewing steak
4 oz (100 g/4 oz) fat streaky bacon
Salt and pepper
Ground mace
7 oz (200 g/7 oz) plain flour (all purpose flour)
A little red wine
Beef stock
3 oz (75 g/3 oz) fat (dripping, margarine and lard or butter and lard)

Using a small, sharp knife, cut the breast meat off the rooks or pigeons in whole pieces, discarding the remainder of the carcass. Arrange the breast meat in a dish, cover it with milk, cover the dish and leave it to steep for 4 to 6 hours or even overnight in the refrigerator. The following day, drain off and discard the milk. Cut the beef steak into even-sized pieces just a little smaller than the breast meat and put it in a pie dish, covering the beef with the rook or pigeon. Remove the rinds from the bacon, roughly chop the rashers and strew them over the meat, seasoning everything with salt, pepper and some ground mace. Sprinkle with 1 oz (25 g/1 oz) plain flour and pour in the red wine and enough stock to cover. Use water if there is neither red wine nor stock available, although the addition of even a little of either to water will give the pie a richer flavour. Cover the pie dish with foil and cook the meat in a moderate oven 350°F (180°C), gas mark 4 for about 1½ hours or until both meats are tender. Remove the dish from the oven and allow it to cool completely.

Meanwhile, make the pastry so that it has time to rest before being rolled out. Sift the remaining flour into a bowl with a good pinch of salt. Cut in the fat then rub it in until the mixture looks like fine breadcrumbs. Mix to a smooth, non-sticky dough with cold water. Wrap the pastry in greaseproof paper and chill it in the refrigerator for at least 30 minutes.

Roll the pastry on a lightly floured board until it is at least 1 in (2.5 cm) larger than the pie dish. Grease the rim of the dish. Cut off a ½ in

(1.25 cm) strip from around the pastry and lay it on the pie dish rim, pressing it gently into place and cutting and joining it. Moisten this strip with cold water and top the pie with the round of pastry. Press the edges to seal them, trim and decorate them.

Bake the pie in a moderately hot oven at 400°F (200°C), gas mark 6 for about 30 minutes or until the crust is a good golden brown. Serve hot with new potatoes or with spring cabbage, cooked until just tender, then drained and finished with butter and pepper.

Potted pigeons   *serves 4–6*

Today we are concerned about the high cost of fuel and its conservation and so recipes such as this have lost favour. Once they were cooked economically by leaving the pot beside the fire or utilizing the heat left in the baker's oven. A modern alternative is to find other dishes which take a similarly long time to cook and put them all in the oven together. This recipe, and method, works well for other meats and is ideal for older, tougher, often tastier, pieces.

3 pigeons
Salt and pepper
Worcester sauce
4 oz (100 g/½ cup) melted butter

Pluck and draw the pigeons or buy them ready for cooking from butcher or fishmonger. Rinse them, put them in a pan, barely covering them with water. Add a lid, jamming it on with a cloth or piece of foil so that the steam cannot escape. Bring to the boil and simmer gently until the meat is falling off the bones (approximately 2½ hours for pigeons). As soon as the meat is cool enough to handle, pick out the bones and return them, with pieces of cartilage, to the stock in the pan to be reduced to approximately ¼ pt (125 ml/½ cup) by hard boiling. Meanwhile, mince the meat finely, season it with salt and pepper and Worcester sauce and moisten it with a little stock. Pack it into small jars or a large dish and smooth the top before running the melted butter over as a seal.

Sauces and Stuffings

Sauce recipes for the most part have been borrowed from other countries, as we have no history of sauce-making of our own, except for those mixtures which the French disparagingly refer to as 'bastard sauces'— apple, bread, mint and custard made with custard powder. We have one masterpiece which is Cumberland sauce, and the true custard, made with eggs, sugar and milk or cream, is wonderful, but probably not of our doing.

However, we excel at stuffings, through economy perhaps, but the end result is still to be applauded. Little wonder, then, that Michael Smith for his book *Fine English Cookery* and Jane Grigson for *English Food* both eked out their chapters on sauces and stuffings with recipes for preserves.

Good gravy *serves 2–4*

It does not matter whether you make gravy to go with poultry, game or meat, because the rules are the same. Begin with a little of the fat left in the roasting tin but more important, use the juice and sediment in the tin, thicken it with flour and use a good matching stock, if you can. If not, do not scorn vegetable water, and, if cooking poultry or game, use the giblets first for stock, then in the gravy for extra flavour, removing them before serving.

1 tbsp (15 ml/1 tbsp) fat and juices from the roasting tin
1 level tbsp (15 ml/1 good tbsp) plain flour (all purpose flour)
Approximately ½ pt (250 ml/1¼ cups) stock or vegetable water
Salt and pepper

For preference, make your gravy in the roasting tin after removing the meat on to a hot plate and pouring off excess fat into a dripping pot, keeping various drippings in separate pots. Stir in the flour with the tin over a gentle heat and use the wooden spoon to scrape crisp bits and pieces off the bottom of the tin. Gradually pour in the stock, bringing the mixture to the boil and thickening it on top of the stove as you go. When all the stock has been added, reduce the heat and simmer the gravy for 5 to 10 minutes, stirring it now and then. Check for seasoning before adding salt and pepper because most stocks and vegetable water will have salt in them. Add some salt and plenty of pepper, freshly ground if possible. Pour, or strain, into a jug or sauceboat for serving.

For onion gravy, finely chop, then boil in salted water, 1 large onion and use the chopped onion and the liquid to make the gravy.

Gravy may be thin or thick but it is traditional to serve a thin gravy with beef, poultry and game and a thicker one with pork and lamb. But as this is a matter for personal preference, adjust the quantities of flour and stock to suit your taste.

Apple sauce   *serves 4–6*

Traditionally for this sauce, we use Bramley apples, a variety which first grew in a Nottingham garden. Apparently the original tree still flourishes in that cathedral city. Lately, the French are teaching us to use eating apples for cooking; something we have resisted for years in the erroneous belief that they were not right. Certainly eating apples were more expensive than cookers, but nowadays, the prices have evened up, so you should try a sauce made of Granny Smiths, Cox's orange pippins, Worcesters or Russets. Serve it with pork, duck or goose.

2 lb (1 kg/2 lb) apples
2 oz (50 g/4 tbsp) unsalted butter
A little ground nutmeg, cinnamon or mace (optional)

Peel, core and chop the apples into even-sized pieces, putting them in a pan with a little water. Bramley's require only a tablespoon or two, because they break down nicely into a smooth purée with little cooking. Firmer varieties such as Granny Smith apples will require more water, but if you find that when the apples are soft, there is too much liquid, pour it away, otherwise the sauce will be sloppy. Ideally when the apples and liquid are mashed, the consistency should be such that a wooden spoon drawn through the mixture leaves a parting for a second or so. If still too liquid, stir the purée briskly over the heat to drive off some of the moisture. Then add the butter, beating it in well. Spice with ground nutmeg, cinnamon or mace and serve hot or cold.

Bread sauce   *serves 4–6*

Another of our simple old English sauces served to accompany roast game and poultry. I don't think much of the simplest recipes which produce a sauce lacking in flavour and with a distressingly gritty texture. This one is rich, spicy and I have to make double quantities to be sure of having some to serve with cold meats.

1 medium onion
4–6 parsley stalks
2 in (5 cm) cinnamon stick
12 black peppercorns

1 whole clove or ½ a small bay leaf
½ pt (250 ml/1¼ cups) milk
6 oz (175 g/3 cups) fine white fresh breadcrumbs
Salt and pepper
4 tbsp (60 ml/⅓ cup) double cream (heavy cream)
A knob of butter
Ground nutmeg or mace

Skin the onion and put it in a pan with the rinsed parsley stalks, cinnamon stick, peppercorns and whole clove or piece of bay leaf. Pour in the milk and bring it slowly to the boil. Remove the pan from the heat, cover it with a lid and infuse as long as possible, even overnight. Next day, strain the milk, returning it to a rinsed pan. Add the crumbs, stirring them well to make a thick sauce, adding more if the consistency is too thin. Cook this mixture very gently for about 30 minutes, stirring frequently. Stir in plenty of salt and pepper and the cream. Taste and correct the seasoning if necessary, and finish the sauce with a good knob of butter and a sprinkle of ground nutmeg or mace.

Cheese sauce   *serves 2–4*

This sauce appears to be used to cover all foods in English rural cookery; today it is probably the most useful sauce for a beginner cook to know.

1 oz (25 g/2 tbsp) butter
1 oz (25 g/4 tbsp) plain flour (all purpose flour)
½–¾ pt (250–375 ml/1¼–scant 2 cups) milk
¼ pt (125 ml/⅔ cup) single cream (light cream)
4 oz (100 g/1 cup) grated cheese
1 level tsp (5 ml/1 good tsp) made English mustard
Salt and pepper

Melt the butter in a pan then stir in the flour and cook the roux gently for 2 minutes, stirring occasionally. Remove the pan from the heat and gradually stir in the milk, using the smaller amount if you want a coating sauce and the larger amount for a pouring sauce. Bring the mixture to the boil, stirring all the time the sauce thickens, then reduce the heat and let the sauce simmer for 4 minutes, stirring it occasionally. Stir in the cream, although this is optional, then stir in the cheese but only until it has melted. Do not continue to cook the sauce once it contains the cheese because this will toughen it, turning it stringy. Season with the mustard and salt and pepper.

   The sauce can be turned into a sauceboat or poured over cooked fish, poultry, vegetables or pasta. If you wish to brown the dish covered in the sauce, sprinkle it either with fine breadcrumbs or with more grated cheese (or you can use a mixture of the two) and put it under a hot grill until golden brown.

Cumberland sauce   *serves 4–6*

This is a masterpiece, but you must use a good, dark red port; tawny and white ports will not give the required colour.

3 medium oranges
3 medium lemons
1 lb (454 g/1 lb) redcurrant jelly
¼ pt (125 ml/⅔ cup) dark sweet port
1 level tsp (5 ml/1 good tsp) mustard powder
Salt and pepper
1 level tsp (5 ml/1 good tsp) very finely chopped onion
A tiny pinch of ground nutmeg
2 tbsp (30 ml/2 tbsp) white wine vinegar

Use a potato peeler to remove the rinds from the oranges and lemons, then inspect each piece of rind and remove any white pith with a small, sharp knife. If you are not scrupulous about this, you will discover bitter tastes in your sauce. Gather the peel into neat piles and cut them into very fine shreds using a small, sharp knife. Michael Smith advises in his book *Fine English Cookery*, first published by Faber and Faber in 1973, that you shred the peel 'as fine as a pin, for this will ensure that your sauce is good-looking and elegant.' He stresses that your patience will pay dividends.

Put the peel shreds in a pan and just cover with water then bring to the boil, strain it at once and refresh the peel under running cold water for a good minute. Finally drain the peel and put it on one side. Squeeze and strain the juice of the oranges and 2 of the lemons, pouring it into a pan. Add the remaining ingredients (save for the peel shreds) and bring the sauce to the boil over a very low heat, stirring it all the time. Simmer for 15 minutes. Add the shreds of peel and simmer the sauce for a further 10 minutes until it begins to thicken. Allow to cool, then chill it and serve it without straining out the pieces.

Mint sauce   *serves 2–4*

The French abhor our habit of serving a sharp mint sauce with lamb. The British remain unrepentant, even helping themselves to mint sauce *and* redcurrant jelly.

1 level tbsp (15 ml/1 good tbsp) finely chopped fresh mint
A tiny pinch of castor sugar
1 tbsp (15 ml/1 good tbsp) white wine vinegar

Mix the chopped mint with the sugar and vinegar to serve. If you prefer a thicker or thinner sauce, adjust the quantities of mint and vinegar accordingly, but always add the tiny pinch of sugar, not so much to sweeten as to bring out the flavour of the mint.

Horseradish sauce   *serves 6–8*

You can buy horseradish sauce or cream in small bottles, a very mild accompaniment indeed. For the real thing, you need to dig up a root, grate it, which will make you cry, and mix it with cream.

1 large horseradish root
Double cream (heavy cream)
Salt and pepper
A little lemon juice

Scrub the root, cutting off the very tip and the top as you would prepare a carrot. Shave off the brown skin; if you can work with the root and peeler under water it will help. Coarsely grate the root, remembering that it loses much of its pungency after grating, so this is best done prior to serving. Stir the shreds into some cream, season the sauce with salt and pepper and lemon juice and keep stirring or whisking to make a thick cream.

Cranberry sauce with orange   *serves 8–10*

Essential for roast turkey dinners.

8 oz (225 g/8 oz) cranberries   2 large oranges
4 oz (100 g/good ½ cup) granulated sugar
1 tbsp (15 ml/1 tbsp) port or sherry (optional)

Pick over the cranberries and put them in a pan. Squeeze out and strain the juice from one orange. Finely grate the rind from the other one, then cut off the remaining peel and pith and cut the segments from their skins with a small, sharp knife. Roughly chop the segments, gathering the juice to add with the squeezed juice to the cranberries. Bring slowly to the boil, cover the pan, and simmer the cranberries for about 7 minutes, or until they are tender but not bursting. Stir in the orange pieces and the sugar until the sugar has dissolved and allow to cool. For extra flavour, port or sherry can be added when the sauce is cold.

Caper sauce   *serves 4*

This is traditional with boiled mutton which is almost impossible to buy these days. Serve caper sauce with boiled lamb, or if made with a fish stock, it may be served with poached fish.

1 oz (25 g/2 tbsp) butter
1 oz (25 g/4 tbsp) plain flour (all purpose flour)
½ pt (250 ml/1¼ cups) stock, lamb or fish
1 level tbsp (15 ml/1 good tbsp) capers
2 tsp (10 ml/2 tsp) white wine vinegar
Salt and pepper

Melt the butter in a pan and stir in the flour, cooking the roux gently for 2 minutes. Gradually stir in the lamb or fish stock and bring the sauce to the boil, stirring it all the time it is thickening. Reduce the heat and simmer for 3 minutes.

Drain the capers and use them whole or roughly chopped, depending on the dish for which the sauce is intended. Stir the capers into the sauce with the vinegar and salt and plenty of freshly ground white pepper. Simmer for 1 minute, check the seasoning and serve in a sauceboat.

Egg custard sauce   *serves 4–6*

1 pt (500 ml/2½ cups) milk
1 vanilla pod

2 oz (50 g/¼ cup) castor sugar
1 level tsp (5 ml/1 good tsp) cornflour (cornstarch)
5 large eggs, size 2

Heat the milk with the vanilla pod to boiling point. Meanwhile, mix the sugar with the cornflour (cornstarch), lightly beat the eggs and beat them gradually into the sugar. Remove the pod from the milk and slowly pour the milk into the eggs, whisking all the time. Return the custard to the saucepan and stir it over a very low heat until the custard thickens smoothly.

Serve the sauce hot, pouring it into a jug. If you wish to serve it cold for trifles, for instance, dip the base of the pan in cold water to prevent the custard cooking further, then press a piece of wet greaseproof paper closely against the surface of the custard and let it cool. The paper will prevent a skin forming as it cools.

Chocolate sauce *serves 2–4*

A rich, dark sauce which can be served hot with steamed and baked puddings or cold with ice cream.

3 oz (75 g/3 oz) Chocolat Menier (good plain chocolate)
2 oz (50 g/¼ cup) castor sugar
2 level tsp (10 ml/3 level tsp) cocoa

Break the chocolate into a saucepan and add the sugar, cocoa and ¼ pt (125 ml/⅔ cup) cold water. Heat gently until the chocolate has melted then simmer the sauce for 3 minutes, stirring occasionally to ensure it does not catch on the bottom. Add another ¼ pt (125 ml/⅔ cup) cold water then bring the sauce to the boil, reduce the heat and simmer it for 20 minutes until it is thick and syrupy. Serve hot or cold.

Orange sauce *serves 2–4*

2 large oranges
2 level tsp (10 ml/3 level tsp) arrowroot (cornstarch)

Using a potato peeler, remove the rind from 1 orange then inspect the peel and cut away any white pith adhering to it. Cut the rind into very fine strips then bring it to the boil in enough cold water to just cover it, drain it and refresh the shreds under running cold water. Drain and pat dry. Squeeze the juice from both oranges and strain it into a small pan. Bring it to the boil. Blend the arrowroot (cornstarch) with a little cold water, then pour in some of the hot juice, stirring all the time, finally returning the mixture to the pan. Bring back to the boil, stirring all the time until the sauce thickens and clears. Add the rinds and simmer the sauce for 2 minutes.

This is a useful sauce to know because this method can be used to thicken any fruit juice, whether tinned, frozen or fresh. To each ½ pt (250 ml/1¼ cups) liquid, use 2 level tsp (10 ml/3 level tsp) arrowroot (cornstarch).

Brandy sauce   *serves 4–6*

In these affluent days, cream has become the sauce to serve with Christmas puddings, but I still prefer the sweetened cornflour sauce regarded by the French as an abomination.

1 oz (25 g/2 tbsp) unsalted butter
1 oz (25 g/4 tbsp) cornflour (cornstarch)
¾ pt (375 ml/scant 2 cups) milk
2 oz (50 g/good ¼ cup) castor sugar
2 tbsp (30 ml/good 2 tbsp) brandy (or rum)

Melt the butter in a pan and stir in the cornflour (cornstarch), then gradually stir in the milk to make a smooth mixture. Bring the sauce to

boiling point, stirring all the time, then lower the heat and simmer it for 3 or 4 minutes, stirring occasionally. Stir in the sugar and on the point of serving, add the brandy (or rum).

Lemon nut stuffing

2 oz (50 g/¼ cup) blanched almonds
1 large lemon
1 oz (25 g/2 tbsp) butter
3 oz (75 g/1¼ cups) fresh white breadcrumbs
1 small egg, size 4 or 5
Salt and pepper

Finely chop the almonds then toast them under the grill, putting them on a piece of foil and shaking them frequently so that they brown evenly without burning. Finely grate the rind from the lemon and squeeze out and strain the juice. Melt the butter then stir in the breadcrumbs and fry them fairly quickly for 2 to 3 minutes, stirring them until they are an even golden colour. Stir in the nuts, lemon rind, juice, beaten egg and salt and pepper and mix well to bind.

This stuffing is good with chicken and pork, also for turkey, but the quantities should be doubled for the larger birds.

Curried rice and apricot stuffing

1 small onion
2 oz (50 g/¼ cup) butter
3 oz (75 g/¾ cup) cooked rice
A good pinch of dried thyme
2 oz (50 g/¼ cup) dried apricots
1 small egg, size 4 or 5
Salt and pepper
1 level tsp (5 ml/1 good tsp) curry powder

Skin and finely chop the onion and fry it in the butter for 5 to 8 minutes until it is golden. Stir in the cooked rice and fry for another 2 minutes, stirring. Add the thyme. Cut the dried apricots into small pieces and stir them into the mixture with the beaten egg, salt and pepper and curry powder, adding only enough of the egg to bind the ingredients together.

Use this stuffing for chicken but double the quantities for a turkey of modest size. A 20 lb (9 kg/20 lb) bird will require as much as 1 lb (450 g/1 lb) weight of stuffing.

Sage and onion stuffing

This is the classic stuffing for pork and goose.

8 oz (225 g/8 oz) onions
Salt and pepper
4 oz (100 g/2 cups) fresh white breadcrumbs
1 level tsp (5 ml/1 good tsp) finely chopped fresh sage
1 oz (25 g/2 tbsp) butter

Skin and quarter the onions and cook them in boiling salted water to just cover them for 15 to 20 minutes until they are almost tender. Drain them (reserve the water for gravy) and chop them roughly; a saucer and a colander should be used for chopping, the edge of the saucer fitting the rounded base of the colander well. Mix them with the breadcrumbs, sage and salt and pepper. Melt the butter and stir it into the stuffing and if it is still a little too crumbly, bind it with a little of the onion water or a little beaten egg.

Puddings

I have never counted them, but there must be as many traditional pudding recipes as there are meat dishes. Certainly they outnumber foreign imports and many of those which we make today and think of as foreign have a version, at least as old, often older, somewhere in England's culinary history. Poor knights of Windsor is called pain perdu in France, crème brulée becomes burnt cream in England and clafoutis turns out to be similar to the sauce batters of the fruit-growing areas of this country.

Whatever disparaging remarks one makes about the Victorian era, one has to admire the inventiveness and energy of the time, and recipes from Eliza Acton, Mrs Beeton and other writers of the era reflect this well. There are dozens of steamed and baked puddings called by the names of towns coming into prominence as the fast-expanding railways made them famous. Manchester, Chester and Newcastle are three such puddings. Alma pudding, Delhi pudding and patriotic pudding were invented to honour victories while Prince Albert pudding showed how much we approved of Queen Victoria's consort; although as it is a steamed, solid pudding made from prunes, was it, instead, a fine joke at the time?

Any number of poor man's or working man's puddings are to be found, showing that we called a spade a spade, and though simple in the number of ingredients used and the style of cooking, most of them are worth trying.

Certain fruits have always grown well in the English garden and although the varieties used by our ancestors bear little resemblance to modern fruits, no doubt, they had more individual flavour. Unfortunately, when sugar became more readily available, the tendency was to over-sweeten puddings; something we still persist in doing.

Apple pie *serves 6–8*

At its simplest, that is sliced Bramley apples and sugar between a double crust and made on a plate, it is a nice dish, but it may be easily improved by adding a few Cox's orange pippins to the Bramleys, or a quince. Cloves and other spices were used in the eighteenth century, but I find whole spices unacceptable, flavouring strongly only the immediately surrounding fruit. Better to use ground spice, mixing it with the sugar and sprinkling it evenly throughout the layers of apples. In Yorkshire, cooks eschewed the spices, preferring the plain pie which they served with cheese; a good combination.

1 lb (450 g/1 lb) Bramley apples
2 or 3 Cox's orange pippins
3 oz (75 g/6 tbsp) castor sugar or to taste
A little lemon juice (optional)
8 oz (225 g/8 oz) shortcrust pastry

Peel, core and slice the apples and toss them in the sugar, adding, if you like, a little lemon juice to sharpen the flavour again. Roll the pastry on a lightly floured board and use half of it to cover a lightly greased tin or enamel plate. Pile the apples on the pastry and moisten the edge of it with water. Cover with the remaining pastry, pressing the edges to seal them. Trim and decorate as you wish. Make a small hole in the centre of the top crust, brush the pie with water and sprinkle it with granulated sugar.

Bake it in a moderately hot oven at 400°F (200°C), gas mark 6 for 20 to 25 minutes for Bramley apples on their own or until the crust is a golden brown. If you add other apples to the Bramleys, or a quince, reduce the temperature after 20 minutes cooking to moderate 350°F (180°C), gas mark 4 and continue cooking for another 20 minutes.

Poor knights of Windsor   *serves 4–6*

Not a recipe which can be claimed solely by the English because the French version, pain perdu, just proves that thrifty cooks in other countries wasted nothing.

Eight $\frac{1}{2}$ in (2.5 cm) thick slices of white bread
$\frac{1}{2}$ pt (250 ml/1$\frac{1}{4}$ cups) milk
2 oz (50 g/4 tbsp) castor sugar
2 large eggs, size 2
2 oz (50 g/$\frac{1}{4}$ cup) butter
Jam

Cut the crusts off the bread. Whisk the milk with the sugar and eggs and pour it into a flat dish. Quickly dip in the bread on both sides, just enough to moisten it, not to soak it. It should not be soggy.

Melt the butter in a large frying pan and fry the bread slices until they are golden brown and crisp on both sides. Quickly spread with jam, cut into fingers if preferred, and serve at once.

Working man's pudding   *serves 4*

We used to be more inventive with few ingredients and poor man's cakes, puddings, knights of Windsor and other dishes were made, often from what was left over or stale. This is a Yorkshire recipe which had to go to

New Zealand with my aunt and come back again for me to appreciate it. Although the mixture is sloppy, it makes a delicious pudding. The cup to use is a ½ pt (300 ml) standard breakfast size.

1 cup of plain flour (all purpose flour)
¼ cup of sugar (brown or white)
1 cup of mixed dried fruit
1 level tsp (5 ml/1 level tsp) ground spice (whatever you have)
1 cup of boiling water
1 level tsp (5 ml/1 level tsp) bicarbonate of soda
1 dessertspoon (10 ml/1 tbsp) margarine or butter

Mix all the ingredients together and beat well. Turn the mixture into a greased pudding basin, cover with pleated foil to allow for expansion and boil the pudding for 2 hours. Serve with custard, jam or cream, although this rather defeats the economical aspect of the pudding.

Raised gooseberry pies   *serves 6*

This is a curious mixture, hot water crust paste and sweetened fruit, but it works well.

4 oz (100 g/½ cup) lard
1 lb (400 g/4 cups) plain flour (all purpose flour)
½ level tsp (2.5 ml/½ level tsp) salt
1 lb (450 g/1 lb) gooseberries
4 oz (100 g/½ firmly packed cup) castor sugar
1 small egg, size 4 or 5

Put the lard with 7 fl oz (195 ml/scant 1 cup) water in a pan and bring it to the boil. Sift the flour with the salt into a bowl and when the water boils, pour it at once into the flour and mix it quickly with a wooden spoon to a dough. As soon as it can be handled comfortably, but do not let it cool completely, knead the dough lightly in the bowl then divide it into 6 pieces. From each piece remove a quarter then mould the larger piece around a floured jam jar, pushing the pastry up the sides of the jar to make a crack-free case about 2 in (5 cm) high. While you work, keep the remaining pastry warm because once it becomes cold it is unworkable. Tie a band of folded greaseproof paper around each case, then ease it off the jam jar. Divide the gooseberries, topped and tailed, into the cases, strew with the sugar and mould the reserved pieces into rounds for the lids, sticking them in place with a little beaten egg. Neaten the tops by snipping round the joins with scissors, make a small hole in the centre of each pie top and decorate the pies if you wish, although by tradition, sweet pies are left plain. Brush with egg.

Bake the pies in a moderately hot oven at 400°F (200°C), gas mark 6 for about 30 minutes until the pastry is beginning to firm, then lower the temperature to moderate 350°F (180°C), gas mark 4 and continue cooking for another hour or so until the pies are a shiny golden brown. Remove the paper bands 15 minutes before the end of the cooking time, brush the pies with the remaining egg and return them to the oven so that the sides can brown.

Serve hot or cold with cream.

Marble sponge pudding   *serves 6–8*

6 oz (150 g/1½ cups) self-raising flour (all purpose flour with raising agent)
6 oz (150 g/¾ cup) butter
6 oz (150 g/¾ cup) castor sugar
3 large eggs, size 2

Milk
1 oz (25 g/4 tbsp) cocoa
A pinch of baking powder

Sift the flour. Cream the butter and sugar until the mixture is light and fluffy. Lightly beat the eggs, then gradually beat them into the creamed mixture, adding a spoonful of the flour with the last additions of egg if the mixture looks as though it might curdle. Fold in the remaining flour, mixing to a soft dropping consistency with milk if necessary. Divide the mixture in half and fold the cocoa and baking powder, sieved together first, into one half.

Use large spoons and alternately put large amounts of plain and chocolate mixture into a buttered 1¾ pt (1 l/4½ cups) pudding basin. Cover with buttered foil or greaseproof paper, pleating it under the rim or securing it with string but allowing it to balloon a little so the pudding has room to rise. Boil or steam the pudding for 2 hours, replenishing the pan with boiling water, not just hot water, whenever necessary.

Turn the pudding on to a hot plate and serve it with chocolate sauce, see page 89.

Rhubarb crumble   *serves 4–6*

Imagine a cook running short of time, the pastry for the rhubarb pie almost ready, rubbed in but not rolled out. You can see her quickly mixing a little sugar into the bowl, perhaps adding a touch of ground spice, piling the crumbs over the fruit and baking it.

2 lb (1 kg/2 lb) rhubarb
4 oz (100 g/good ½ cup) granulated sugar
6 oz (150 g/1½ cups) plain flour (all purpose flour)
3 oz (75 g/scant ½ cup) unsalted butter
3 oz (75 g/scant ½ cup) castor sugar

Wash the rhubarb, cut it into 2 in (5 cm) lengths and pack it into a pie dish, sprinkling each layer with granulated sugar. Sift the flour into a bowl, rub in the butter and stir in the castor sugar. Cover the rhubarb with the crumble mixture but do not pack it down, simply strew it on.

Bake the crumble in a moderately hot oven at 375°F (190°C), gas mark 5 for 30 to 45 minutes or until it is golden brown. If it looks as though it will be too brown by the time it is needed, turn the oven temperature to moderate 350°F (180°C), gas mark 4 and cook the crumble for longer.

Unlike pastry, crumble mixtures are very good-natured and will stand a longer slower cooking and, if necessary, being kept warm.

Bakewell tart or pudding   *serves 6*

The original shop is there in Bakewell, Derbyshire, still producing the tart, sometimes called a pudding. The exact recipe is supposed to be a secret, and perhaps the original is, but today's commercialization of puddings means that anyone who wishes to make Bakewell tart at home can certainly produce one with as fine a flavour as any that come from Derbyshire.

8 oz (225 g/8 oz) shortcrust pastry
3 level tbsp (45 ml/4 level tbsp) raspberry jam
4 oz (100 g/½ cup) unsalted butter
4 oz (100 g/good ½ cup) castor sugar
3 large eggs, size 2
4 oz (100 g/1 cup) ground almonds

Allow frozen pastry to thaw for at least an hour or make fresh pastry, rolling it on a lightly floured board and using it to line a 9 in (23 cm) shallow pie dish. Trim and decorate the edges, then spread with the jam.

Cream the butter and sugar until light and fluffy, lightly beat the eggs then add them to the creamed mixture a little at a time, beating well. Fold in the almonds and spread the mixture over the jam, smoothing the top. Bake it in a hot oven at 450°F (230°C), gas mark 8 for 5 minutes then lower the temperature to fairly cool at 300°F (150°C), gas mark 2 and continue cooking for 40 to 45 minutes until the top is golden brown and springy when pressed lightly in the centre. Serve hot or cold.

Apple and almond pudding   *serves 4–6*

This is a glorious pudding, simple in looks as are so many of the best English puddings, subtle and delicious in flavour.

2 lb (1 kg/2 lb) Cox's orange pippins
1 level tbsp (15 ml/1 good tbsp) honey
2 oz (50 g/1 cup) fresh white breadcrumbs
Rosewater
3 oz (75 g/scant ½ cup) butter
3 oz (75 g/scant ½ cup) castor sugar
3 oz (75 g/good ¾ cup) ground almonds
Grated rind of 1 lemon
1 large egg, size 2
1 oz (25 g/4 tbsp) flaked almonds

Peel, core and slice the apples into a pan with 4 tbsp (60 ml/5 tbsp) cold water. Simmer the fruit very gently until it is soft then beat in the honey, breadcrumbs and some rosewater, about 2 tsp (10 ml/2–3 tsp) to flavour. Turn the mixture into a shallow ovenproof dish, 1¾ pt (1l/4½ cups) size.

Cream the butter and sugar until light and fluffy, stir in the ground almonds and lemon rind then beat the egg and beat it into the mixture. Spread this over the apples to cover them, sprinkle with the flaked almonds and bake the pudding in a moderate oven 350°F (180°C), gas mark 4 for about 40 minutes or until the top is risen and golden brown. Serve with plenty of cream.

Fruit fools   *serves 4*

Gooseberry and apricot are the fruits most often used in recipes from old cookery books and in the past fools were marbled puddings, delicately swirled rather than beaten to a uniform colour. The fruit was recognizable, mashed rather than sieved to a smooth purée.

1 lb (450 g/1 lb) fruit such as gooseberries, apricots, peaches or the soft
  fruits
2 oz (50 g/4 tbsp) granulated sugar
½ pt (250 ml/1¼ cups) double cream (heavy cream)

Prepare the fruit, topping and tailing, stoning or hulling. Gooseberries, apricots, peaches or other slightly hard fruits will require a light cooking until tender but still fairly whole, adding the sugar and only enough water to make a soft but not too liquid mixture. Mash lightly with a fork. The soft fruits will simply require a light mashing, adding the sugar as you mash.

Lightly whip the cream then fold in the fruit and serve the fool, chilled, in glasses.

Less extravagant fools can be made with egg custard, custard made from custard powder or a mixture of either of these with a little cream.

Summer pudding   *serves 6*

The English have a surprising number of puddings which use bread, none finer or more delicious than this one. It is essential to use a good bread. Wrapped sliced bread gives the pudding an unpleasant slippery texture.

2 lb (1 kg/2 lb) soft fruits, raspberries, red-, white- or blackcurrants,
strawberries, loganberries or early blackberries
3 oz (75 g/scant ½ cup) castor sugar
8 slices of white bread

Choose a mixture of soft fruits, pick them over and put them in a saucepan

with the sugar. Cover the pan and simmer the fruit over a very low heat, shaking the pan occasionally to make sure the mixture is not catching on the bottom of the pan. Five minutes should be enough to soften the fruits and for the juices to run freely. Allow to cool completely, then pour off the juice into a separate bowl or soup plate.

Cut the crusts off the bread and cut the slices to fit the pudding basin, narrowing each one slightly at one end. Cut a circle for the base. All of these will be on show when the pudding is turned out, so make them neat; the bits and pieces can be used for the top. A 1¾ pt (1 l/scant 4½ cups) basin is about the right size. Soak each piece of bread in the fruit juice before putting it in position, then fill the basin with the fruit. Soak the bread for the top, pour the remaining juice over the fruit and cover it with the rest of the bread.

Choose a small plate or saucer for the top, making sure it is small enough to sit inside the basin rather than on top. Add a weight from your scales or large tins of fruit and leave the pudding in a cool place overnight, turning it on to a serving plate the next day.

Serve the pudding decorated with fresh fruit and with a good spoon of softly whipped cream on top.

Bread pudding   *serves 8–9*

When my packed lunch for school contained a couple of squares of bread pudding, I was very popular for swapping. Bread and dripping came a close second.

1 lb (450 g/1 lb) stale bread
8 oz (225 g/8 oz) mixed dried fruit
3 oz (75 g/¾ cup) chopped fresh suet
¼ level tsp (1.25 ml/¼ level tsp) salt
2 oz (50 g/6 tbsp) chopped mixed peel (optional)
1 level tsp (5 ml/1 level tsp) ground cinnamon
½ level tsp (2.5 ml/½ level tsp) ground nutmeg
3 oz (75 g/½ cup) soft brown sugar
1 large egg, size 2
A little milk

Tear the bread into small pieces. Cover the bread with cold water and leave it to steep for 40 minutes. Squeeze the bread as dry as you can between your hands, put it in a large bowl and beat in the remaining ingredients, mixing well. Transfer the mixture to a buttered 8 in (20 cm) square cake tin and smooth the top. Bake the bread pudding in a moderately hot oven at 375°F (190°C), gas mark 5 for 2 to 2½ hours or until the top is crisp and golden brown.

Leave it in the tin until quite cold, cut it into large squares, sprinkle with castor sugar and serve. If you want to serve bread pudding hot, cut squares, lift what you want from the tin, sprinkle them with sugar and serve with custard.

Apple tansy   *serves 4*

The tansy is a perennial plant associated with Easter when the bright green leaves were baked in a custard of eggs, sugar, milk and flour to be eaten on Easter Sunday. The tansy has given its name to some custard dishes, even though they do not contain the leaves. If you have tansy in the garden, you could add some to a custard just to experience the bittersweet flavour.

½ pt (250 ml/1¼ cups) double cream (heavy cream)
½ level tsp (2.5 ml/½ level tsp) ground mace
A pinch of ground mixed spice
1 oz (25 g/1 oz) boudoir biscuits
2 large eggs, size 2
2 large egg yolks, size 2
2 oz (50 g/¼ cup) castor sugar
1 large cooking apple
1 oz (25 g/2 tbsp) butter
1 tbsp (15 ml/1 tbsp) lemon juice

Pour the cream into a pan and add the mace and mixed spice. Crush the biscuits to fine crumbs and add them to the pan. Heat gently until the mixture is warm, stirring it all the time. Beat the eggs and egg yolks into the pan with half of the sugar and cook the mixture over the lowest heat for about 5 minutes, stirring it all the time. Remove the pan from the heat.

Peel and core the apple and cut it into ½ in (2.5 cm) rings. Melt the butter in a large frying pan and fry the apple rings on both sides for 3 minutes just to soften them slightly. Pour in the cream, reduce the heat and cook the tansy gently for 10 to 15 minutes or until the underside is golden brown. Turn it out of the pan inverting it on to a plate and return it to the pan, to cook the other side. Fry gently for another 10 or 15 minutes until golden.

Turn the tansy on to a hot serving plate, sprinkle it with the lemon juice and strew with the remaining sugar. Serve at once.

Chester pudding   *serves 6*

At the mixing stage this pudding is an odd blue colour, rather offputting, I know, but it becomes an appetizing brown during the cooking.

4 oz (100 g/1 cup) self-raising flour (all purpose flour with raising agent)
4 oz (100 g/2 cups) fresh white breadcrumbs
4 oz (100 g/1 cup) chopped fresh suet
2 oz (50 g/¼ cup) castor sugar
6 oz (150 g/1½ cups) blackcurrant jam
5 tbsp (75 ml/6 tbsp) milk

1 level tsp (5 ml/1 good tsp) bicarbonate of soda
A pinch of salt

Mix the flour, breadcrumbs and suet in a bowl. Make a well in the centre, add the sugar and 4 oz (100 g/1 cup) of the jam. Warm the milk slightly but do not let it boil then stir in the bicarbonate of soda and salt, pour this mixture at once into the bowl and mix very well to a stiff dropping consistency. Transfer it to a buttered 1¾ pt (1 l/4½ cups) pudding basin and cover it with buttered foil, pleating it under the rim or securing it with string, but allowing it to balloon a little so that the pudding has room to rise. Steam or boil the pudding for 2 hours.

　Heat the remaining jam with a little cold water, turn the pudding out of its basin, pour on the jam sauce and serve at once.

Lemon love cake　*serves 6*

A disparaging remark about school dinners on my recent television series was not ignored. I was quickly taken to task and bombarded with menus. Most of the ideas were for well-balanced fare of the kind to be expected, but one pudding name stayed in my mind and I asked for the recipe. Lemon love cake (in proportions for fifty children) needed scaling down to feed six people and on testing proved to be a lovely lemony shortcake sandwich and a perfect example of how British food is evolving yet retaining its British characteristics.

6 oz (175 g/¾ cup) margarine
6 oz (175 g/¾ cup) castor sugar
1 medium egg
12 oz (350 g/3 cups) plain flour (all purpose flour)
2 tsp (100 ml/2 tsp) baking powder
A pinch of salt
1½ tbsp (40 ml/2 tbsp) lemon curd

Cream the margarine and sugar thoroughly then beat in the egg. Sift in the dry ingredients, stirring until the mixture looks like large bread-crumbs with no loose flour visible. Gather the mixture together, kneading until the consistency is right for rolling. Chill for 30 minutes. Roll half the dough on a lightly floured surface to a round slightly smaller than an 8 in (20 cm) straight-sided, loose-bottomed sandwich tin. Put the round in place in the greased tin and press down into the tin as for shortbread.

　Spread with lemon curd leaving a ½ in (1.25 cm) border. Roll the remaining mixture, place it on top and seal the edge well, then decorate it. Bake the cake in a moderate oven at 350°F (180°C), gas mark 4 for 45 minutes or until golden and risen. Cool for a few minutes in the tin before turning it out. It is fragile when hot. Serve warm or cold.

Baking

Breads were the first baked goods, originally unleavened, later raised with yeast. Cakes came much later, maybe as much as thousands of years later, beginning simply enough as part of the batch of bread dough enriched with dried fruit and sugar, a legacy which survives today in regional specialities such as the lardy cakes of Wiltshire, the west country's saffron cakes, Yorkshire teacakes and barmbracks which indicate by their title that the original yeast of ale barm was used in their making.

During the early nineteenth century, reputedly made fashionable by the Duchess of Bedford, society took to tea drinking as a mid-afternoon occasion when it was essential that Cook should produce as many varieties of dainty sweet and savoury foods as the social status of the household demanded. The Victorians, consumers of large amounts of food at all times of the day, also insisted on a mid-morning refreshment. Madeira, the wine discovered in the island of Madeira and brought home by British shippers, was very popular, accompanied by pieces of plain cake as a relief from the rich, sweet drink. Sand cakes, pope lady cakes and Madeira cake were the correct offering.

This time coincided with the development of a raising agent, a powder which could produce lighter cakes than those raised with yeast or eggs alone, thus contributing to the great English tradition of cake-making but speedily causing the demise of the more substantial yeast cakes.

Now as we watch our weight with a universal zeal, tea as a meal is being forgotten, except in the north of England where tea has always been a late-evening meal, rather more substantial than that served in the nineteenth century. For the farmers and industrial workers alike, tea marked the end of the day and was essentially full of calories. No dainty slices of bread and butter rolled into fine cylinders or prettily decorated cakes; instead thick bread and dripping or other fat, slabs of cake with sweet, strong tea, all preceded by the kind of savoury that is as appropriate at lunch.

Making bread

Large households always baked enough bread for their needs as did farmers' wives and women who lived in rural areas. It was only in urban areas that bakers began to set themselves up to produce bread and buns for workers to buy. And their large bread ovens were used, once the bread was baked, to slowly cook jars of meat and vegetables for the bakers' neighbours. They would pay him pennies for the heat, collecting the jar of succulent ingredients later in the day.

Originally everyone made wholemeal bread, using the complete wheat grain, ground between two large stones. The bread was coarse with bran, dark and fairly heavy in texture. The industrial revolution introduced white flour, so called because the darker and most nutritious particles were sifted out, although the 'white' flour would have been more of a beige colour. White bread, more expensive because of the extra process, was eaten by the bosses, and longed for by the largely penniless workers. Now we have come full circle and wholemeal bread is the fashion amongst those with the money to pay for it and the knowledge to recognize that white breads are good for nothing. But whichever flour you use for bread-making, the method is the same, except you should note that wholemeal flour will absorb more liquid than white flour.

1 lb (500 g/4 cups) strong flour (bread flour)
Salt
½ oz (15 g/1 tbsp) fresh yeast or ½ this quantity of dried yeast
Approximately ½ pt (250 ml/generous 1¼ cups) tepid water

Sift the flour with the salt into a large, warm bowl. Cream the yeast (if fresh) with a teaspoon in a cup until it is liquid. If you are using dried yeast, sprinkle the granules on most of the tepid water and leave it for 15 minutes or so until it forms a sponge on top. Make a well in the flour and pour in the creamed fresh yeast mixed with most of the tepid water, or pour in the dried yeast liquid. Gradually mix in the flour, drawing it from the walls around the well into the liquid until you have a smooth, soft dough. It should not be sticky. If it is, it requires a little sprinkling of flour and a mental note to add a little less water next time you are making bread. If it is too dry, add a very little water and continue kneading the dough in the bowl until it feels elastic and forms one large ball, leaving the sides of the bowl clean.

There is no need to change bowls or make more washing up by using extra equipment; simply sprinkle a little flour over the ball of dough and cover the bowl with a tea towel wrung out in hot water. Stand the bowl in a warm place and leave it for 1 to 1½ hours. The usual temperature of a domestic kitchen is ideal for bread dough, but the dough will rise even in the refrigerator. From this you can see that bread dough just needs time and if after 1½ hours the dough has not doubled in size, leave it alone for a while longer until it looks well puffed, smooth and stretched like a balloon. Knock back the dough with your fist, knead it a couple of times in the bowl then turn it on to a lightly floured board and continue to knead it hard for 4 or 5 minutes which will develop the gluten (so the loaf will keep a good shape during baking), distribute the yeast evenly and start it working hard again to raise the dough.

Grease a 2 lb (1 kg/2 lb) loaf tin with oil or lard and form the dough into an oblong to fit the tin. Make sure the top is smooth by pulling any creases to the bottom of the dough and folding the dough underneath itself to create a perfect fit for the tin. The dough, at this stage, will half fill the tin, so cover it with a warm cloth, a damp cloth, and leave it in a warm place until the dough has expanded and risen to the top of the tin. This is where the long efforts of kneading are repaid. Well kneaded dough will quickly rise again in the tin, achieving a greater volume (and a more even loaf) than an indifferently kneaded dough.

Bake the loaf in a hot oven at 450°F (230°C), gas mark 8 for the first 15 minutes to kill the yeast and set the shape of the loaf, then reduce the oven temperature to moderately hot at 400°F (200°C), gas mark 6 for another 15 to 25 minutes, then remove the loaf from its tin and return it to the oven for a final 5 minutes cooking. When perfectly baked, it will have a rich golden brown top crust and sound hollow when tapped underneath with the knuckles. Let the loaf cool completely before putting it in the bread bin or wrapping it for the freezer. Even so the crust will soften a little but not as much as it does if put away hot.

If you have a large mixer with a dough hook, use this to knead the dough both before and after the initial rising. If you wish to increase the quantities to make 2 or 3 loaves, do not increase the quantity of yeast, whether fresh or dried. This amount of yeast will raise up to 3 lb (1½ kg/

3 lb) of flour. Be particularly sparing in your measurements of dried yeast. Too much produces a dry dough, and I think most modern bread recipes are over-generous with it to the detriment of the finished product. If by some mistake you eventually mix in less yeast than a recipe suggests, a long slow rising (or even two) will give the smaller amount of yeast the time to raise the dough as you would like.

Crumpets   *makes 16*

I have always called crumpets pikelets which seems to be a north country dialect word. Muffins were never in my vocabulary because we never ate them, so I was never confused and the round, flat yeast cakes with holes in the top simply became crumpets when I moved south. So I was amazed by the confusion which does exist and refer you to Elizabeth David's book *English Bread and Yeast Cookery*, which goes into the whole subject most thoroughly. Like Mrs David, I have tried crumpet recipes galore trying to find a finished product less rubbery and clammy to the touch than the commercially prepared objects on sale. Many times, I gave up and bought from my baker who makes much thicker crumpets than those bought in packets. This always brings on waves of nostalgia similar to choosing eggs and putting them in a paper bag rather than an egg box. While my mis-shapen crumpets have certainly tasted better than those I bought, too thin a batter has run into the pan from the crumpet rings, while too thick a batter which stays where it is put, doesn't have holes on top when cooked. Finally, I worked out the following recipe which is always successful and which produces a good-looking result.

8 oz (225 g/2 cups) strong plain white flour (bread flour)
8 oz (225 g/2 cups) ordinary plain white flour (all purpose flour)
½ oz (15 g/1 tbsp) fresh yeast or ½ this quantity of dried yeast
generous 1 pt (600 ml/almost 3 cups) half milk to water
2 level tsp (10 ml/2 level tsp) salt
1 level tsp (5 ml/1 level tsp) castor sugar
½ level tsp (2.5 ml/½ level tsp) bicarbonate of soda
¼ pt (125 ml/⅔ cup) warm water

Sift the flours together into a bowl. Cream the fresh yeast with a teaspoon in a cup. If you are using dried yeast, sprinkle it on to the mixed milk and water which should be heated to blood temperature for either yeast. Leave the dried yeast for 15 minutes or so until it forms a spongy top. Make a well in the centre of the flour. Mix the fresh yeast with the warmed milk and water and pour it into the flour or pour in the dried yeast liquid. Add the salt and sugar and beat the batter very hard with a wooden spoon or an electric mixer until it is smooth. Cover with a tea towel wrung out in hot water and leave the batter for 1½ to 2 hours at room temperature to rise. The whole surface will be covered with bubbles when ready. Beat the batter down to its original size with the wooden spoon. Dissolve the bicarbonate of soda in the warm water and stir it into the batter. Cover the bowl again and leave the batter in a warm place for about 30 minutes to rise again.

To cook the crumpets, grease a heavy frying pan or a girdle, grease some crumpet rings (these are not easy to find so use plain pastry cutters made of metal) and stand them slightly apart in the pan. Pour in enough batter to come almost to the top of the rings and cook them fairly slowly for 7 to 10 minutes until the top of each crumpet is a mass of small holes. Once the crumpets are fairly firm and the top is set, remove the rings and turn each one over for another 2 or 3 minutes' cooking. If you find the top surface of the first batch is not covered with tiny holes after cooking, thin the batter with a little more warm water before cooking the next batch.

Mrs David's recipe taken from Walter Banfield's book *Manna* published in 1973, includes 2 tbsp (30 ml/2½ tbsp) oil and she notes that having made crumpets with and without the oil which is an unorthodox addition, those made without oil are thinner, having less volume and flavour. Try it and see what you think.

Lardy cake   *serves 6–8*

Traditional to Wiltshire and other southern counties, although there are versions from almost every district, this once celebration cake was made from a batch of plain bread dough, saved during bread-making and enriched with pork fat, spices and dried fruit. It has a lot in common with Chelsea buns, hot cross buns, Yorkshire spice loaves, the Guernsey gache, the barabrith from Wales and the barmbrack, the Irish version of the barabrith.

8 oz (225 g/2 cups) plain flour (all purpose flour)
1 level tsp (5 ml/1 level tsp) salt
½ oz (15 g/1 tbsp) fresh yeast or ½ this quantity of dried yeast
1 large egg, size 2 or 3
¼ pt (125 ml/⅔ cup) warm milk
2 oz (50 g/¼ cup) pure pork lard
2 oz (50 g/¼ cup) castor sugar
2 oz (50 g/¼ cup) sultanas

Sift the flour and salt into a warm bowl and keep the flour warm while you prepare the yeast. Fresh yeast simply requires creaming to a liquid using a teaspoon to work the yeast against the sides of a cup. Dried yeast should be sprinkled on half of the warm milk and left for 15 minutes or so until it forms a sponge on top. Make a well in the centre of the flour, pour in the creamed fresh yeast mixed with half of the warmed milk or the dried yeast and warmed milk. Gradually work the flour into the liquid, adding more of the warmed milk (although you may not need it all) until you have mixed a soft but not sticky dough. Knead this dough fairly well, first in the bowl until it becomes elastic and leaves the sides of the bowl clean, then on a lightly floured work surface for 4 or 5 minutes. Return the dough to the clean bowl, sprinkle the top of the dough with a little flour and cover the bowl with a tea towel wrung out in hot water. Leave the dough in a warm place for about 1 hour or until it has doubled in bulk. Punch the dough down again, knead it well and roll it with the minimum of flour until it is a good oblong. Divide the lard, sugar and sultanas into 3 portions and cover two-thirds of the dough with one-third of the filling ingredients. Fold the dough in thirds as you would for puff pastry, the plain third over the middle and the final third over the top to sandwich the filling ingredients between the layers of dough.

Turn the dough so the layered side is towards you, roll it again to an oblong, cover with filling ingredients and fold it as before. Repeat with the final portion of lard, sugar and sultanas, then roll it and fold it twice more, finally shaping the folded dough with your hands to fit an 8 in (20 cm) round, deep cake tin by folding the corners underneath and so forming a round. Cover the tin with the damp tea towel and leave the dough to rise to the top of the tin, which, in a warm kitchen, usually takes about 30 minutes. Bake the lardy cake in a hot oven at 450°F (230°C), gas mark 8 for 30 to 35 minutes or until it is golden brown and well risen. Finally remove the cake from the tin and turn it upside down and put it back in the tin to let the lard soak through to the crust. Cut into slices, serve hot and well buttered. A rich, rib-sticking cake, not for everyday fare, but as a once in a while sweet treat.

Scones   *makes 8*

Originally cooked on a bakestone, or girdle, over an open fire, these small scones which we serve with jam and butter, or clotted cream in the south-west, have many variations. The simplest recipe, given here, can be made fruity with the addition of dried fruit. Savoury scones, made by stirring in grated mature strong-flavoured cheese, can also be served with butter, jam or extra cheese, but whichever you decide to make, serve them freshly cooked and warm. Scones stale quickly which can be disguised a little by heating day-old scones in the oven before serving them, but there is no substitute for straight from the oven to the tea table.

8 oz (225 g/2 cups) plain flour (all purpose flour)
2 level tsp (10 ml/1 level tbsp) baking powder
½ level tsp (2.5 ml/½ level tsp) salt
2 oz (50 g/¼ cup) butter
¼ pt (125 ml/⅔ cup) milk

Sift the flour thoroughly with the baking powder so that the baking powder is well distributed. Mix in the salt. Because baking powders are a mixture of bicarbonate of soda with cream of tartar mixed with rice flour, cornflour, arrowroot or potato flour to prevent the alkaline and acid ingredients beginning to work before they are needed, and because the proportions of bicarbonate of soda to cream of tartar to the stabilizing ingredient vary from one manufacturer to another, be guided by the quantities suggested on the tin. The amount specified here is an average amount required for scones. Rub the butter into the dry ingredients to make a mixture which looks like fine breadcrumbs, then gradually mix in the milk to form a soft but not sticky dough. Turn the dough on to a lightly floured board and work rapidly and lightly, kneading the dough until it is free of cracks. Roll the dough to a ½ in (1.25 cm) thickness and using a cutter, cut rounds. With a 2½ in (6 cm) fluted cutter, after re-rolling the small pieces, you will be able to make eight scones. Transfer them to a lightly greased baking sheet, brush the top of each one with milk and bake them in a hot oven at 450°F (230°C), gas mark 8 for about 10 minutes until they are golden brown and well risen.

Sultana scones

Stir 1 oz (25 g/3 tbsp) castor sugar and 2 oz (50 g/6 tbsp) dried fruit into the mixture before adding the milk.

Wholemeal scones

Use the recipe given above but substitute wholemeal and brown flours, half and half of each, for the white flour.

Soda scones

If you prefer to work with bicarbonate of soda and cream of tartar rather than with a commercially prepared baking powder, use 1 level tsp (5 ml/1 level tsp) cream of tartar and ½ level tsp (2.5 ml/½ level tsp) bicarbonate of soda instead.

Buttermilk scones

If you add buttermilk instead of fresh milk, it contributes some of the acid required (in proportion with the alkaline bicarbonate of soda) to raise the scones, so you must reduce the cream of tartar by half. In this recipe, ½ level tsp (2.5 ml/½ level tsp) is required plus the same amount of bicarbonate of soda. Soured milk and treacle also supply acid and if using these, again you need to reduce the quantity of cream of tartar by half.

Cheese scones

Strong-flavoured cheese, approximately 2 oz (50 g/6 tbsp) cheese should be finely grated and stirred into the dry ingredients before the milk is added. Omit any sugar, of course.

Pope lady cake   *serves 8*

Cakes have become richer and sweeter and many of the plain cakes which were popular because they were the ideal accompaniment to something rich (such as the plain Madeira cake so called because it was handed round with glasses of Madeira) are rarely made these days. Pope lady cake is a pale-coloured sponge, light textured and with a fine flavour, which can be dressed up or not as you please. I can find no reason for its curious title, having discovered the recipe first in a book of old traditional recipes published by Whitbread, the brewers, in the mid-fifties. I have only a photocopy of the book which omits the title pages. *British Cookery*, edited by Lizzie Boyd, containing a different version, attributes it to Hertfordshire and divides it between two sandwich tins. I prefer this version, cooked as one deep cake.

6 oz (175 g/⅔ cup) unsalted butter
8 oz (225 g/1 cup) castor sugar
8 large egg whites, size 2
6 oz (175 g/1½ cups) plain flour (all purpose flour)
3 oz (75 g/scant ½ cup) cornflour (cornstarch)
½ level tsp (2.5 ml/½ level tsp) baking powder
1 tsp (5 ml/1 tsp) lemon or almond essence or rosewater

Cream the butter and sugar with 4 of the egg whites until the mixture is light and fluffy. Sift the flour, cornflour (cornstarch) and baking powder together and fold them into the mixture. Whisk the remaining egg whites until they are very stiff and fold them into the mixture with the lemon or almond essence or rosewater for flavour. Turn the mixture into an 8 in (20 cm) deep round cake tin, greased and lined with greased greaseproof paper. Bake the cake in a cool oven at 300°F (150°C), gas mark 2 for about 1½ hours or until it is well risen, golden, shrinking slightly from the edges of the tin and springy to touch. Cool on a wire rack and serve as a plain cake, or split it and layer it with a filling.

Rich chocolate cake   *serves 6–8*

Spain and Portugal held the lands where the cacao tree grew and so chocolate was a closely guarded ingredient until more than a century after the conquistadors discovered it. By degrees it was introduced into the rest of Europe but it was not until the early nineteenth century that it was mass-produced into the block form so familiar today. Chocolate cakes, then, are a recent addition to English fare and recipes range from a little cocoa added to a Victoria sponge cake at the plain end of the spectrum to cakes made by melting real chocolate and mixing it with other fine ingredients. It is unfortunate that many of the chocolate confections we buy are not real chocolate at all but flavoured mixtures, chocolate coloured. The chocolate to buy for good cakes where you are using liqueurs, unsalted butter and other fine ingedients is called Chocolat Menier; a large thin bar encased in a white and green wrapper.

Two 3½ oz (100 g/3½ oz) bars Chocolat Menier (good plain chocolate)
6 oz (175 g/⅔ cup) unsalted butter
2 tbsp (30 ml/2 tbsp) Cointreau or Grand Marnier
4 eggs, size 2
6 oz (175 g/⅔ cup) castor sugar
1 level tbsp (15 ml/1 level tbsp) finely grated orange rind
1 oz (25 g/4 tbsp) cornflour (cornstarch)
3 oz (75 g/¾ cup) plain flour (all purpose flour)
Whipped cream
Fresh cherries, cream and chocolate curls to decorate

For this recipe, pre-heat the oven to moderate 350°F (180°C), gas mark 4 and have ready two 8 in (20 cm) sponge sandwich tins, greased and lined on the bases with greased greaseproof or non-stick paper. Ideally, the tins

should have loose bases so that this rich cake can be freed from the tins without damage.

Break the chocolate bars into small pieces and put them in a large basin with the butter, cut into small pieces. Stand the basin over a saucepan containing gently simmering water, but make sure the base of the bowl is above the water and that the chocolate does not become too hot. Leave until the chocolate has melted, then mix it thoroughly with the butter adding the liqueur. Break the eggs into another large bowl, add the sugar and whisk until the mixture is light and fluffy. It will require a good 5 to 10 minutes beating before it will hold a trail for 5 seconds after you lift the whisk from the mixture. Fold in the chocolate mixture and orange rind. Sift the cornflour (cornstarch) with the plain flour (all purpose flour) and lightly fold it through the mixture in two batches. Divide between the tins and smooth it gently and evenly. Bake the cakes in the oven for about 30 minutes until they are well risen, springy to the touch and shrinking slightly from the sides of the tins. Put two large tins of fruit on the work surface and use one to push up the base of each cake tin. When the cakes have cooled a little you can move them to the safety of a cooling rack. Sandwich the cakes with whipped cream and decorate the top with cream, fresh cherries and curls of chocolate. The cakes have a sugary crust.

Moggy   *serves 8*

I know nothing of this recipe, where it comes from, how it gets its name, but I include it for two reasons. I think the cake is delicious and I have a particular fondness for the non-pedigree cats affectionately called moggies!

1 lb (450 g/1 lb) self-raising flour (all purpose flour with raising agent)
1 tsp (5 ml/1 tsp) bicarbonate of soda
1 tsp (5 ml/1 tsp) ground ginger
A pinch of salt
½ lb (225 g/1 cup) light brown sugar
5 oz (125 g/⅔ cup) margarine   *Milk to mix*
½ lb (225 g/generous ⅔ cup) golden syrup   *1 large egg, size 2*

Sift the flour, bicarbonate of soda, ground ginger and salt and mix it with the sugar in a bowl. Make a well in the centre. Gently heat the margarine with the golden syrup until the margarine has melted. Add it to the bowl and mix well with a little milk and with the lightly beaten egg. You should have a soft consistency. Turn the mixture into a greased and lined 8 in (20 cm) square cake tin and bake the cake in a moderate oven at 325°F (160°C), gas mark 3 for 1 to 1¼ hours until it has risen, shrunk slightly from the edges of the tin and is springy to touch. Allow the cake to cool completely before you remove it from the tin then store it in an airtight tin. Moggy is best when kept for 1 week before being cut.

Working man's cake   *serves 6*

This is the cake version of working man's pudding, see page 95.

1 oz (25 g/2 tbsp) butter
12 oz (375 g/3 cups) plain flour (all purpose flour)
3 level tsp (15 ml/3 level tsp) baking powder
1 tsp (5 ml/1 tsp) salt
6 oz (175 g/⅔ cup) sugar   Milk
4 oz (100 g/½ cup) mixed dried fruit   1 egg

Rub the butter into the flour which has been sifted with the baking powder and salt. Add the sugar and dried fruit and mix the dough to a stiff consistency with the milk and egg. Shape it on a floured board into a round tea cake. Then bake on a tray for 30 to 40 minutes in a moderate oven, at 350°F (180°C), gas mark 4.

Oatcakes   *makes 15*

With today's emphasis on natural foods and the inclusion of bran in our diets, oatcakes, those slightly bitter-tasting biscuits which are such hard work to eat, are to be found in most shops. Despite their thinness, oatcakes are a substantial food, 2 or 3 being plenty with cheese for lunch. Those I knew in Yorkshire (I associate the biscuits with Scotland) were thicker, softer, more cake-like and fried with bacon for breakfast, or served buttered for tea.

8 oz (225 g/1¼ cups) pin-head or fine oatmeal
8 oz (225 g/2 cups) plain flour (all purpose flour)
½ level tsp (2.5 ml/½ level tsp) salt
1 oz (25 g/2 tbsp) fresh yeast or ½ this quantity of dried yeast
½ pt (250 ml/1¼ cups) warm water

Sift the oatmeal and flour with the salt into a warm basin and while activating the yeast, put the bowl in a warm place to take the chill off the flour. Cream fresh yeast with a teaspoon against the sides of a cup, using a little of the warm water to help the process. If using dried yeast, sprinkle it on top of the warm water then leave it for 15 minutes or until it forms a sponge-like mass on top. Mix the remaining water with the fresh yeast. Make a well in the dry ingredients and pour in the yeast liquid, gradually working in the flour mixture from the sides and beating all the time to make a thin smooth batter. You may have to add a little more warm water. Grease a heavy frying pan or a girdle and pour batter on it to form one large round as is traditional in some parts of the country, or four smaller rounds each about 2 in (5 cm) in diameter. Cook each oatcake for about 3 minutes on the first side, then for about 1 minute after they have been flipped over. Eat them well buttered, hot from the pan. Those that are left may be fried with the bacon in bacon fat or dripping for breakfast, or toasted to be spread with good beef dripping and seasoned with a little salt and plenty of pepper.

Potato oatcakes　*makes 8*

If you like an even softer oatcake, use potatoes as the binding ingredient.

1 lb (450 g/1 lb) freshly boiled potatoes
6 oz (150 g/1 good cup) pin-head or fine oatmeal
1 level tsp (5 ml/1 level tsp) salt
Milk or buttermilk to mix

Drain and dry the potatoes over a gentle heat and mash thoroughly or make sure there are no lumps at all by pushing them through a sieve. Mix in the oatmeal and salt, but only if the potatoes were cooked without salt, then add enough milk or buttermilk (or soured milk or soured cream—either of which is marvellous in oatcakes) to make a stiff dough. With some potatoes it will not be necessary to add liquid; add it only if the dough is unworkable. Turn the dough on to a lightly floured board, knead it lightly until it is smooth, then roll it to a $\frac{1}{4}$ in ($\frac{1}{2}$ cm) thickness and cut it into rounds using a 3 in (7.5 cm) cutter. Prick each one all over and cook them in a heavy frying pan or on a girdle, lightly greasing the surface for each oatcake. Flip each one over as soon as the underside is light golden brown. Serve hot and buttered for breakfast or supper, and always freshly cooked. As with the yeast oatcakes, those which aren't eaten straight from the pan may be fried or toasted later.

Christmas cake　*serves 10*

The recipe exists in the eighteenth century and before as plum or plumb cake, or rich cake, but this particular super-fruited mixture did not specifically become a Christmas cake until about the middle of the nineteenth century. Mrs Beeton includes recipes for Christmas cakes, Mrs Rundell in 1810 does not. In her book *A New System of Domestic Cookery* she suggests how to make a very fine cake of butter washed with water first, then with rosewater, beaten with 20 eggs, fruit and sweetmeats cut fine, for over 1 hour. Today's recipes while still very rich, have reduced the hard work.

8 oz (225 g/1 cup) butter
8 oz (225 g/1 cup) soft dark brown sugar
6 large eggs, size 2 or 3
1 small lemon
$\frac{1}{2}$ level tsp (2.5 ml/$\frac{1}{2}$ level tsp) ground mixed spice
$\frac{1}{2}$ level tsp (2.5 ml/$\frac{1}{2}$ level tsp) ground cinnamon
$\frac{1}{2}$ level tsp (2.5 ml/$\frac{1}{2}$ level tsp) ground cloves

5 level tbsp (75 ml/6 level tbsp) black treacle
1 lb (500 g/1 lb) plain flour (all purpose flour)
12 oz (375 g/2 cups) large raisins
8 oz (225 g/1¼ cups) sultanas
8 oz (225 g/1¼ cups) currants
3 oz (75 g/⅓ cup) glacé cherries
Orange juice
1 level tsp (5 ml/1 level tsp) bicarbonate of soda
4 tbsp (60 ml/5 tbsp) brandy

Cream the butter and sugar until the mixture is light and fluffy. Separate the eggs and beat the yolks, one at a time, into the creamed mixture. Finely grate the rind from the lemon and squeeze out and strain the juice. Beat the rind, juice, spices and black treacle into the creamed mixture. Sift the flour and alternately fold it into the mixture with the dried fruit, adding a little orange juice to make the mixture just workable. It should be very stiff at this point because the egg whites and brandy have still to be added. Blend the bicarbonate of soda with a little orange juice and stir it into the mixture, then whisk the egg whites until they are stiff and fold them in alternately with the brandy, until you have a stiff dropping consistency.

Turn the cake mixture into a greased and lined 9 in (23 cm) round cake tin with a loose base and bake it towards the bottom of a slow oven 275°F (140°C), or gas mark 1 for 3 to 4 hours until the cake is brown and firm to the touch. Check that it is cooked right through by pushing a warm skewer down into the centre. It should be clean when withdrawn, so if there is cake mixture adhering to it, return the cake to the oven for extra cooking.

This is a lovely moist cake, fruity but not densely heavy as some cakes can be. Ice it with marzipan and royal or fondant icing.

Marzipan

More properly this should be called almond paste. Marzipan was once a fairly solid cake called St Mark's pain (French for bread) then marchpane, hence marzipan.

8 oz (225 g/2 cups) ground almonds
8 oz (225 g/1 cup) castor sugar
8 oz (225 g/2 cups) icing sugar   *1 tsp (5 ml/1 tsp) lemon juice*
2 large egg yolks, size 2   *Apricot jam or clear honey*

Mix the ground almonds with the castor sugar then sift in the icing sugar and mix again thoroughly. Add the egg yolks and lemon juice and mix to a stiff paste, which should be workable and fairly easy to knead smooth but not so soft that it leaves your hands oily. Work it on an icing sugar-strewn board or work surface until it is smooth, free of cracks and pliable, then roll just over half of it into a long strip for the sides; the remainder should be rolled into a circle for the top. Brush the sides with apricot jam, or with clear honey which, unlike the jam, doesn't require heating and sieving and press the strip around the edge, cutting and smoothing the join. Press the circle on top and neaten all edges, making them square and removing finger marks by rolling a straight-sided jar or tin around the edge, and the rolling pin lightly across the top.

Royal icing

2 large egg whites, size 2
1¼ lb (550 g/5 cups) icing sugar

½ tsp (2.5 ml/½ tsp) lemon juice
1 tsp (5 ml/1 good tsp) glycerine

Lightly beat the egg whites in a large bowl until they are foamy, then gradually sift in and work in the icing sugar with the lemon juice and glycerine to prevent the icing setting to a cement-like hardness. Beat the mixture all the time and continue to beat for 5 to 8 minutes after all the icing sugar has been added. The icing should stand up in stiff points and be very white and glossy when it has been beaten enough. Ideally, store the icing overnight in a polythene box with a good airtight lid. This will give air bubbles time to disperse. Then spread the icing over the top and sides and peak it for a snow effect, or if you wish to have a smooth icing, spread icing first on top and draw a ruler across the top surface to make it smooth. Ice the sides and turn the cake against the edge of the ruler to smooth the sides. Apply another coat of icing for a really smooth finish, using a fine sandpaper between the coats to smooth any rough patches. If necessary, sandpaper the final coat. Allow to dry, then pipe icing around the edges. Icing left after coating the cake can be used for piping if you keep it in a polythene box with an airtight lid and store it in the refrigerator.

Decorate the cake with Christmas figures and greetings and encircle with a ribbon, or with a cake frill, although these are not so popular nowadays. A pity, I like them.

Fondant icing

1¼ lb (550 g/1¼ lb) icing sugar
1 large egg white, size 2
1 tbsp (15 ml/1 good tbsp) glucose syrup

Sift the icing sugar into a large bowl, add the egg white and glucose syrup and knead the mixture together to form a smooth icing. Roll it on a work surface, lightly covered with sifted icing sugar, until it is large enough to completely cover a 9 in (23 cm) cake. Smooth it over the cake, making sure it is free of creases. Trim the bottom edge smooth and decorate it with piped royal icing.

If you cannot find glucose syrup in your local chemist, use golden syrup, although this will make a creamy-coloured icing.

Gingerbread   *serves 8–10*

Dorothy Hartley in *Food in England* first published in 1954 describes the oldest gingerbread as a solid slab of honey, flour, ginger and other ingredients, popular as a gift in the 'tournament' period, when it was decorated with box leaves and cloves, gilded with gold leaf, and resembled a piece of tooled and studded leather. Later, figures made of a gingerbread biscuit mixture were gilded and sold at fairs and spring and harvest celebrations. No doubt, many of these figures were kept rather than eaten, particularly if they were a love token, and with constant handling, the gilding wore away, hence the popular phrase, 'that takes the gilt off the gingerbread'. Dorothy Hartley gives instructions for pressing gold leaf on to gingerbread, and even though a little goes a long way, I suppose most of us would balk at eating something so costly, even though, like silver leaf used in celebration Indian cookery, it is harmless. This is my favourite gingerbread recipe; the cake is dark, moist and fairly substantial.

8 oz (225 g/1 cup) butter
4 oz (100 g/½ cup) soft dark brown sugar
8 oz (225 g/¾ cup) black treacle
½ pt (250 ml/1¼ cups) dark ale
1 lb (450 g/4 cups) plain flour (all purpose flour)
A pinch of salt
½ level tsp (2.5 ml/½ level tsp) bicarbonate of soda
2 level tsp (10 ml/2 level tsp) ground ginger
2 level tsp (10 ml/2 level tsp) ground mixed spice
½ level tsp (2.5 ml/½ level tsp) ground cloves
8 oz (225 g/1 good cup) sultanas or mixed dried fruit
4 oz (100 g/½ cup) chopped mixed peel

Cream the butter and sugar until the mixture is light and fluffy. Mix the treacle with the ale and sift the flour with the salt, bicarbonate of soda, ground ginger, mixed spice and cloves. Alternately fold the flour into the creamed mixture with the treacle and ale, adding the fruit and peel with the last additions. Turn the mixture into a greased and lined 10 in (25 cm) square cake tin and bake it in a moderate oven at 350°F (180°C), gas mark 4 for 1 to 1½ hours or until it is well risen and the centre is springy when pressed lightly with a finger. Allow the gingerbread to cool for 15 to 20 minutes in the tin, before turning it on to a wire rack to complete the cooling. In common with all gingerbreads, keep it in an airtight tin for at least 3 days before slicing, when it will have become moister.

Singin' hinnies *serves 4–6*

This recipe comes from Peggy Howie's book published in 1971 called *The Geordie Cook Book*, and the singin' hinnie is so called because the butter and cream sizzles, or sings, on the hot girdle.

½ lb (225 g/2 cups) plain flour (all purpose flour)
2 oz (50 g/¼ cup) butter
2 oz (50 g/¼ cup) lard
1 oz (25 g/3 tbsp) currants
1 level tsp (5 ml/1 level tsp) baking powder
½ level tsp (2.5 ml/½ level tsp) salt
Milk and sour cream

Sift the flour into a bowl and rub in the butter and lard. Stir in the currants, baking powder and salt until well mixed, then add enough milk and sour cream to form a soft but not sticky dough. Knead lightly and quickly on a lightly floured work surface, roll the dough into a large round and bake it on both sides until golden brown on a lightly greased girdle. This takes about 20 minutes. A pair of singin' hinnie hands were used to turn the scone to prevent it breaking. Fish slices are not large enough. It is a slightly unwieldy but effective process to put a plate over the scone and invert both plate and hot girdle together so that the scone drops on to the plate. Then it should be slid off the plate back to the girdle with the golden brown underside now on top. If you prefer, cut the singin' hinnie into halves or quarters for cooking which makes turning each piece easy. Spread with butter, sprinkle with sugar and serve it straight from the girdle.

Preserving

Keeping foods from one season to another was an essential part of survival in England prior to freezers, refrigerators and other modern methods of preservation. At best, a cold place was all that was available which kept meats fresh for a week at the most, but even so the winter months must have been lean ones for many.

Salt was discovered to be a preservative and so were spices, but before this knowledge was commonplace, most people must have eaten rarely, gorging themselves when fresh food was available, or eating rotten foods. However, alcohol is one gain from the natural fermentation of grains, badly stored and allowed to become wet; the raw intoxicating liquor no doubt providing some comfort to the very hungry. Mincemeat owes its origins to an early form of preservation. Once it contained minced meat, spiced heavily and moistened with fat, but gradually the need and the taste for spiced meat has been lost and what remains is the delicious mixture of fruits, spices and suet which is now essential for Christmas feasting.

Although salting played a large part in preservation as late as Victorian times, it has fallen out of favour because there are other and better methods of keeping vegetables, in particular, and the taste and texture of salted, steeped and cooked produce is not acceptable any more. Instead, we turned to bottling and chutney-making as the science of food was investigated. Nowadays, even bottling is loosing popularity because fruits and vegetables can be tucked into the freezer more easily and quickly and with little loss of flavour, colour and texture.

Jam will continue to be a popular method of home preservation because its flavour is superior to commercial jams; chutney- and pickle-making for similar reasons. As we become more conscious of saving money, there is a return to making syrups, rich in Vitamin C, and often made inexpensively from fruits which are available to all who take the time to search the hedgerows.

Some preserving methods are frankly luxurious, but immensely enjoyable in preparation and in eating the results of one's labours. In particular, small perfect apricots, covered in brandy, counter-pointed for colour and flavour with small, whole almonds and packed into pretty jars, are very satisfying. The elderflower champagne recipe I give here is new to me, although when I looked into its origins, I found many similar recipes in old cookbooks, kitchen notes and diaries. My first experimental batch produced a light, almost scented, refreshing drink with a touch of alcohol. My second batch was divided, some for drinking, some for storing to see how it fared.

Because the recipe relies on the natural yeasts present on the elderflowers, the results differ widely and every bottle is a surprise. After six months' storage, it is marvellous with a teasingly elusive flavour of grapes. It is most rewarding to reveal that such a wonderful concoction is the result of a thrifty gathering of flowers on a warm day in May.

Apple, pear and quince jam   *makes 10 lb (4½ kg/10 lb)*

Last year I staggered off the plane from Toronto, Canada, under the weight of 13 lb (6 kg/13 lb) of quinces in my hand baggage. Quince fruit is sold everywhere in Canada in October, whereas it is a rarity in this country, only available to those lucky few who have an old tree in the garden. The flavour of quince is magnificent and one fruit can be used with two or three times its weight of apples or pears in a pie to delicious effect, or to make this jam.

2 lb (1 kg/2 lb) cooking apples
2 lb (1 kg/2 lb) cooking pears
1½ lb (750 g/1½ lb) quinces
1 large lemon
6 lb (3 kg/6 lb) granulated sugar

Peel and core the fruits and cut them into small pieces, the quinces smaller than the apples and pears. Keep the cores and peel and put them on a piece of muslin. Squeeze out and strain the lemon juice. Add the peel, pips and flesh from the lemon to the muslin and tie the contents in a bag shape. Put the chopped fruit in a large pan with 2 pt (1¼ l/5 cups) cold water and the muslin bag and simmer gently until the pieces of quince are completely tender. Remove the muslin bag and squeeze the juices back into the pan. Stir in the sugar, allow it to dissolve, stirring occasionally, and when it has completely dissolved, add the lemon juice and boil the jam rapidly to a set. Test by putting a little of the mixture on a cold saucer, and if after cooling, it wrinkles when pushed with a finger, the jam is ready for potting. Remove the pan from the heat while you test so that the jam does not continue boiling once setting point has been reached. Not only is this wasteful but the jam could catch and burn on the bottom of the pan. Let the jam cool in the pan for 15 minutes then stir it well to distribute the fruit pieces and pour it into hot, dry jam jars. Cover the jam with a waxed disc and the jar with a Cellophane cover, secured in place with a small elastic band. Screw-top jars which once held jam are ideal for re-use provided the lids are undamaged and will make a good seal. If using these, pot the jam, cover the surface with a waxed disc and immediately screw the lid in place. It will form a vacuum as the jam cools and produce a good seal. Label and store the jam in a cool, dark place.

Lemon curd   *makes approximately 4 lb (1¾ kg/4 lb)*

This old-fashioned favourite is not a good keeping preserve; it should be eaten within two or three months if you store it in a cool cupboard, or five or six months if kept in the refrigerator. However, I have always found that matching the supply to the demand is, if anything, the problem, rather than trying to eat up leftovers. Using this basic recipe other curds can be made. Orange and grapefruit curd are delicious, and lime curd, because of the expense of the fruit, is a luxury.

6 large lemons
8 large eggs, size 2
12 oz (350 g/1½ cups) unsalted butter
2 lb (900 g/2 lb) castor sugar

Thinly pare the rind from the lemons, then check each piece of rind, cutting off any white pith. This applies to all the citrus fruits; the pith is bitter and should not be used for making this preserve. Squeeze out and strain the juice. You should have ½ pt (250 ml/1¼ cups) juice so use more or less fruit to achieve this amount. Beat the eggs in a large bowl then add the butter, cut into small pieces, the sugar, lemon rind and juice. Stand the bowl over a pan of gently simmering water, making sure the base of the bowl is above the water level. Or use a double boiler. Cook the mixture gently, whisking all the time until the butter has melted and the sugar dissolved. Strain the mixture through a nylon sieve into a clean bowl, discarding the lemon rind and egg white threads. Then continue to cook the curd over the pan of water, for about 1 hour until the mixture thickens, stirring frequently. The finished texture resembles rich cream. You will find it thickly coats the back of the wooden spoon when it is ready for potting. Pour it into dry but warm jars, cover and label.

Raspberry or strawberry freezer jam
makes approximately 3½ lb (1½ kg/3½ lb)

This is an excellent uncooked jam, preserving the full flavour of the delicate soft fruits, and one of the best uses of the modern-day convenience, the freezer. This jam is runnier than a cooked preserve, but it is set enough to stay where it is spread. Blackberries, plums, apricots, peaches and cherries can be preserved by this means.

1 lb (500 g/1 lb fruit)
2 lb (900 g/2 lb) castor sugar
1 tsp (5 ml/1 tsp) lemon juice
4 fl oz (100 ml/½ cup) liquid pectin

Thick-skinned fruits such as apricots, peaches and plums should be skinned and stoned. Stone the cherries. Then all fruit should be mashed to a pulp with the sugar and lemon juice. Mash according to the consistency of the fruit used; apricots, peaches, plums and cherries requiring more than the soft fruits which really need only to be mashed lightly. Leave the mixture for about 20 minutes, stirring occasionally to make sure the sugar has dissolved and when it has, stir in the pectin and mix thoroughly. Turn the jam into small plastic containers, leaving space for expansion, seal and label but leave the jam at room temperature for 6 to 8 hours. Transfer it to the refrigerator for 1 or 2 days or until it has set, then freeze it. These jams can be stored for up to 12 months, and for use, allow to thaw overnight in the refrigerator, then stir well.

Bullace jam *makes approximately 10 lb (4½ kg/10 lb)*

Few of these old trees survive today and the fruit, which is small, is often overlooked even by the most voracious hedgerow hunter of free food. The bullace is the stock from which all our modern plums were cultivated. You will find the blue-black fruits more often than the greenish variety (which looks like a very small greengage) and because the fruit is more sour than the juicy sweet varieties we now use, they are usually left on the trees until the first frosts have softened their acidity. This recipe can be used for modern varieties of plums and greengages, also for damsons, although the juicier the fruit the less water is required for the initial cooking.

6 lb (2.75 kg/6 lb) fruit
1 pt (500 ml/2¼ cups) water
6 lb (2.75 kg/6 lb) granulated or preserving sugar

Rinse the fruit and remove the stalks. Halve and stone the large varieties. If you do find a bullace tree and the fruits are small, they are almost impossible to stone; you must skim off the stones during the later cooking. Put the fruit in a preserving pan with the water and bring it to the boil over a high heat, then reduce the heat and simmer the fruit for 15 to 30 minutes, depending on the variety, until soft. In the case of the bullace, some of the stones will be freed during this initial cooking and should be skimmed off the top with a slotted spoon. Make sure the fruit skins are soft before stirring in the sugar because they do not soften after the sugar has been added. Stir over a gentle heat until the sugar has dissolved, then raise the heat and boil the jam vigorously until setting point has been reached, usually about 10 to 20 minutes for these fruits with a high pectin content and good setting qualities. Remove free-floating stones with a spoon during cooking. Turn the jam into hot, clean, dry jars, cover and label and store in a cool place.

Elderberry and apple jam   *makes 10 lb*
(4½ kg/10 lb)

There is no need to pick each and every berry off its tiny stalk. The simplest method is to use a fork to strip the stalks. I sit on the floor surrounded by old newspapers, a bag for berries in front of me and the bag of newly picked berries to one side. Ripe berries part quite easily from their stalks when persuaded by the fork and can bounce around the room, hence the paper-covered carpet. If large stalks get into the bag, retrieve them, but a few small stalks in the jam are unnoticeable.

4 lb (2 kg/4 lb) elderberries
1½ lb (750 g/1½ lb) cooking apples
6 lb (3 kg/6 lb) granulated sugar

Put the elderberries in a large preserving pan. Peel, core and finely chop the cooking apples, aiming for 1½ lb (750 g/1½ lb) after preparing them. Add the apples to the pan with ½ pt (250 ml/1¼ cups) cold water. Bring to the boil then simmer the mixture until the fruit is quite soft. Add the sugar, allow it to dissolve, stirring occasionally, then when it has completely dissolved, boil the mixture rapidly to setting point, testing for a set as described in apple, pear and quince jam. Pour the jam into hot, dry jars straight away, cover and label.

Making a jelly preserve   *makes approximately 4 lb (1¾ kg/4 lb)*

Any fruit can be made into a jelly, but this recipe is particularly useful for the hedgerow finds which can include sloes, wild blackberries, often called brambles, rowan berries, barberries and elderberries. From the garden use quince or japonica fruits, mulberries, black- or redcurrants, cultivated blackberries, either alone or mixed with apples.

Jelly recipes always make a point of telling you about jelly bags, the slow drip of juice, everything spanking clean, all of which is important to produce the kind of clear sparkling jelly you would wish to exhibit in a local competition or harvest festival display. However, for your own store-cupboard, the more homely equipment described here is perfectly adequate, gives a good if sometimes slightly cloudy result, but most important is simple to use.

4 lb (1¾ kg/4 lb) fruit
1 pt (550 ml/2½ cups) water
Granulated or preserving sugar

Simply rinse and pick over the fruit to remove insects and damaged berries. There is no need to strip berries of their stalks, particularly useful for small fruits such as elderberries. Put the berries in a preserving pan with the water, bring them to the boil then reduce the heat and simmer gently for 45 minutes, perhaps even 1 hour until the fruit is very soft. Mash it occasionally during the cooking.

I use a contraption of my own making for homely jellies which involves lining a colander with two or three layers of muslin (or clean closeweave cloth instead) and suspending it over a large bowl so that the juice can drip through overnight undisturbed. Another method I find useful is to pour the contents of the saucepan into the cloth in the colander standing in a large bowl, then I gather the corners and tie them to make a bag which I hang above the bowl. However, this latter method does give a cloudier jelly than the former.

Whichever method you use, once the contents of the pan have been poured into the straining cloth, they should be left alone. Stirring or pressing the juice through the cloth will cloud the finished preserve. Measure the juice back into the saucepan and for each 1 pt (600 ml/ 2½ cups) juice, stir in 1 lb (450 g/1 lb) sugar. The contents of the cloth should be discarded. Heat the mixture slowly, stirring frequently until the sugar has completely dissolved, then as for jam, bring to a rapid boil and boil until setting point has been reached. Pot, cover and label.

Herb jellies   *makes 7 lb (3 kg/7 lb)*

An abundance of apples, after some have been frozen as a purée and some used to bulk out scarcer berries such as brambles, can be made into herb-flavoured jellies to serve with meats. Mint and apple jelly is the obvious beginning, but then you can try rosemary jelly, also delicious with lamb, sage jelly for pork dishes, thyme jelly, and also lemon balm or lemon thyme for use as a tea-time preserve.

5 lb (2¼ kg/5 lb) tart apples
1 pt (600 ml/2½ cups) water
4 tbsp (60 ml/5 tbsp) fresh herbs
8 fl oz (250 ml/1 cup) malt vinegar
Granulated or preserving sugar
Green food colouring (optional)

Rinse the apples and pick them over, cutting out any bruises and bad portions, although there is no need to remove stalks, peel or cores. Simply chop the apples into rough pieces and put them in a preserving pan with the water and three-quarters of the herbs. Bring the mixture to the boil, reduce the heat and simmer the fruit for up to 1 hour or until it is really soft and pulpy and mashes easily. Then add the vinegar and boil the mixture for 5 minutes. Strain the juice through several layers of muslin, letting it drip through undisturbed. Then discard the pulp and measure the juice back into the cleaned preserving pan. To each 1 pt (600 ml/ 2½ cups) juice, add 1 lb (450 g/1 lb) sugar and heat gently, stirring occasionally, until the sugar has completely dissolved. Then bring to the boil and boil briskly for about 10 minutes without stirring until the jelly has reached setting point. Skim off any foam with a slotted spoon, sprinkle with the remaining herbs and some green food colouring if you like, adding about 4 or 5 drops for this amount of jelly. Stir well to distribute the herbs and colouring and turn the jelly into warm, clean, dry jars. Cover, seal and label.

Whole sprigs of herbs may be used instead of the chopped herbs for the final flavouring, pushing a sprig into each jar of hot jelly before sealing it.

Marmalade   *makes approximately 10 lb (4½ kg/10 lb)*

Investigate the history of many foods and those with the most English of pedigrees turn out to be foreigners. Thus it is with marmalade which Theodora Fitzgibbon's excellent book, *The Foods of the Western World*, suggests derives from the Portuguese word for quince—marmelo—since quince jelly was the original marmalade. It is now a preserve made from bitter oranges, although in other European countries, marmalade is the word used to describe what we call jam. Theodora Fitzgibbon goes on to describe a Scottish legend which associates the preserve with Mary Queen of Scots. 'It is said that, when ill, she frequently asked for an orange preserve she had been fond of in France. It became known at her court as "Marie-malade", and marmalade is thought by many Scottish people to be a corruption of those words'. Fact or fancy, we do not know, but it is certain that the Scots make good marmalade, particularly the Dundee, prepared by the Keiller family since the eighteenth century and deservedly world-famous.

Of these two recipes, the first is for a light-coloured, thin shred, jelly marmalade; the second for a dark, rich, coarse-cut preserve.

3 lb (1½ kg/3 lb) seville oranges
4 pt (2½ l/5 pt) boiling water
2 large lemons
6 lb (3 kg/6 lb) granulated or preserving sugar

Remove the rind from the oranges and lemons using a sharp, small knife, then cut the rinds into fine shreds, cutting away thick pieces of pith. Cut the oranges and lemons in half and squeeze out and strain the juice. Tie the pips, any pieces of pith removed from the shredded peel and the orange and lemon halves, cut into small pieces, in a large piece of muslin.

Put the shreds of peel with the juice in a large preserving pan and pour on the boiling water. Add the muslin bag and bring it to the boil, then simmer the mixture for 1 to 1½ hours or until the shreds of peel are tender. Remove the pan from the heat, scoop out the muslin bag, suspending it over the pan until it is cool enough for you to squeeze it hard to extract all the liquid. Measure the liquid in the pan and to each 1 pt (600 ml/2½ cups) liquid add 1 lb (450 g/1 lb) sugar. Stir the mixture over a gentle heat until the sugar has completely dissolved, then bring to a rapid boil and continue boiling fast for 20 to 25 minutes or until setting point has been reached, testing for a set before pouring the marmalade into hot, clean, dry jars. Cover, seal and label.

Dark, rich coarse-cut marmalade
makes approximately 10 lb (4½ kg/10 lb)

2 lb (1 kg/2 lb) seville oranges
2 large lemons
6 pt (3½ l/7½ pt) cold water
6 lb (3 kg/6 lb) granulated or preserving sugar
3 tbsp (45 ml/4 tbsp) black treacle

Cut the oranges and lemons in half and squeeze out and strain the juice, reserving the pips. If the white pith is very thick, pare some of it off the orange and lemon rinds and tie it with the pips in a piece of muslin. Cut the remaining peel and pith into fairly coarse shreds. Put the juice, shreds and muslin bag of pips and pith in a large preserving pan with the water, bring it to the boil, then reduce the heat and simmer the mixture for 1½ to 2 hours or until the shreds of peel are tender. Remove the bag of pips and when cool enough to handle squeeze it dry. Add the sugar and treacle and stir the marmalade over a gentle heat until all the sugar has dissolved, then increase the heat and bring the mixture to a fast boil. Continue boiling rapidly for 20 to 25 minutes until setting point is reached. Allow the marmalade to cool in the pan for 15 to 20 minutes or until a skin has formed on the surface, then stir it thoroughly to distribute the shreds of peel. Turn the mixture into hot, clean, dry jars. Cover, seal and label.

Rosehip syrup   *makes approximately 1¾ pt (1 l/2¼ pt)*

Syrups are not so popular a preserve since we seem to have less and less leisure time. And there's no doubt they do take time and they need care during the final preservation process to make sure they keep well. But offsetting this with the fact that the fruit is free for the gathering, you have a cheap preserve, rich in Vitamin C, ideal for drinking when diluted or for serving as a sauce with ice cream, puddings and pies.

3 pt (1¾ l/3¾ pt) water
2 lb (1 kg/2 lb) rosehips
1 lb (450 g/1 lb) granulated or preserving sugar

Wash the rosehips. Bring half the water to the boil in a large preserving pan then mince the rosehips straight into the pan. Stir well, bring back to a rolling boil, then remove the pan from the heat and allow the mixture to cool. Pour it through several layers of muslin (as for a jelly), allowing the juice to drip through. Then return the pulp to the pan, adding the remaining water. Bring slowly to the boil and pour this mixture through the muslin, rinsed clean first. Again allow to drip undisturbed. Pour the two lots of juice into the cleaned preserving pan and boil it hard to reduce it by half. Lower the heat, add the sugar, stirring to make sure it has completely dissolved before bringing the mixture again to the boil. Boil for 5 minutes. Pour the syrup into small screw-top bottles (those which once held mixers for spirits are ideal) leaving about 1 in (2.5 cm) headroom. Screw on the caps tightly. Then turn them back slightly to loosen.

Stand the bottles on wadded newspaper in a pan deep enough to hold water up to the necks of the bottles. Push newspaper between the bottles and the sides of the pan to prevent them touching each other or the metal during the sterilizing process. Bring the water slowly to simmering point and maintain this simmer for a good 30 minutes. If you have a thermometer, it should read 170°F (77°C) throughout the sterilizing. Remove the bottles, fully tighten the screw-tops and allow to cool, then dip each one in melted candle wax for a completely air-tight seal, making sure the wax covers at least 1 in (2.5 cm) of the neck below the screw-tops.

Once opened the syrup keeps for about 2 weeks in the refrigerator so it is advisable to use small bottles.

Sloe gin

Wear gloves when you pick sloes, the round blue-black hedgerow berries which grow on sharply spined trees. Turn them into a jelly to serve with lamb, pork or the Christmas turkey, or use them to flavour gin. When preparing my first bottles of sloe gin, I was advised to stand them by the telephone, which makes more sense than it seems. Each time you make a call or answer the phone, shake the bottles, a necessary part of making sloe gin, with the telephone as an excellent reminder. As a life-long hater of the telephone, I liked this advice; it gave me a good reason for using the wretched instrument.

Sloes
Preserving or granulated sugar
Gin

Pick over the sloes, using only the most perfect for this recipe, and remove any stalks. Prick them all over; I use a darning needle. Pack them in bottles up to the shoulders (if you want to make a lot of this preserve), or, for a trial, pack some into a small jam jar to the three-quarters full point. Top up with sugar. Slowly pour in some gin to the very top and leave for at least six months, shaking the bottle every time you pass it.

Sterilize and dry some bottles then pour the sloe gin through several layers of muslin lining a large sieve, squeezing the pulp to extract all the liquid. Finally pour your sloe gin into the bottles and seal them with screw-caps or with corks, brushing the tops of the corks well with melted candle wax to give an air-tight seal. Keep the gin for at least six months before drinking or giving as presents. Not a quick preserve to make but worth the wait.

Fruits preserved in alcohol

The simplest preserving method of all, although the alcohol makes it expensive, but luxurious to give and receive. Because it is unnecessary to use the finest quality alcohol, look for cheaper bottles of sherry, brandy or whisky. The fruits, however, must be in perfect condition and it is important to choose attractive containers, whether glass or pottery. The only stipulation for a container is that it has an air-tight lid otherwise the alcohol will evaporate in storage. A sad waste.

*Fat prunes, small apricots, small peaches, raspberries, mandarin orange
    segments*
Alcohol (sherry, brandy, whisky, vodka—whichever you prefer)

Fill each jar to the brim with the chosen fruit, pricking the harder fruits such as apricots and peaches with a darning needle so that the alcohol will permeate the flesh. If you wish, you can add whole almonds, slivers of lemon or orange peel or sticks of cinnamon or cloves. Add sufficient alcohol to just cover the fruit and screw on the lid tightly. Leave for 1 week until the fruit has absorbed some of the alcohol then top up the jars. This is particularly important with prunes. Then store the jars for at least

two months before eating, checking them occasionally to make sure the alcohol is still covering the fruit.

Delicious as a pudding or as an addition to ice cream. If there's some of the alcohol left after all the fruit have been eaten, it can be added to trifles or used as a sauce for other puddings.

Elderflower champagne   *makes 1 gal (4½ l/10 pt)*

Some elderflowers have a most unpleasant smell which is not always apparent as you pick them. For this reason it is best to pick a few more heads of flowers than you require and from as many different trees as possible. Once in the bag, those flowers which smell disagreeably can be easily identified and thrown out. Use sweetly scented flowers to make this deliciously refreshing drink or to add a muscat grape flavour to gooseberry jam. Six rinsed heads tied in muslin will flavour 10 lb (4.5 kg/10 lb) jam.

6–12 heads of elderflowers in full bloom
1 large lemon
1¼ lb (550 g/1¼ lb) granulated sugar
1 tbsp (15 ml/1 tbsp) white wine vinegar

Put the elderflowers into a large plastic bucket and pour in 1 gal (4½ l/10 pt) cold water. Pare off the lemon rind, cutting away any pith which has come away with the rind. Squeeze out the lemon juice. Add the rind and juice to the bucket with the sugar and vinegar and cover it with a clean tea towel. Allow the flowers to steep for 24 to 48 hours before straining the liquid into screw-top bottles. Those which held fruit juice are ideal. Keep the drink for 14 days before you try it. It should have a slight fizz as the natural yeasts on the flowers begin to form alcohol from the sugar. From this time, keep the bottles in a cool place.

Pickled onions

There are no quantities to this recipe, because you cover as many pickling onions as you can stand preparing at any one time with enough salt, then with enough spiced vinegar, fitting the results into jars, rather like a three-dimensional jig-saw puzzle. I recommend you prepare at least 2 lb (1 kg/2 lb) pickling onions as a minimum, however.

Pickling onions   *Cooking salt*
Boiling water   *Spiced vinegar (see page 134)*

Cut a thin slice from the root end of each pickling onion then drop them, unpeeled, into a large bowl. Cover them with boiling water and leave them for 1 minute. Drain the onions, pour on cold water and remove them one by one to peel off the skins. Layer the peeled onions as you prepare them in a deep bowl with cooking salt, adding a good layer of salt on top. Cover the bowl and leave the onions overnight. Next day, rinse the onions thoroughly, drain and dry well. Now pack the onions into jars, fitting large ones with small ones to get as many onions as possible into each jar. Pour in sufficient spiced vinegar to cover the onions in each jar. Seal the jars, making them air-tight so the vinegar does not evaporate during storage. Label if you like, although this is not necessary unless you have used different spice mixtures for the spiced vinegar and wish to compare the results. Store the onions in a cool, dark place.

Spiced vinegar

Spiced vinegar is an essential ingredient for most pickles; it can also be used for chutneys. If you make several pickle varieties, it is worth while making a large quantity of spiced vinegar because it can be returned to its original bottles and kept for a month or so.

4 pt (2½ l/5 cups) vinegar
½ oz (15 g/1 tbsp) whole allspice
½ oz (15 g/1 tbsp) whole cloves
1 in (2.5 cm/1 in) piece cinnamon stick
½ oz (15 g/1 tbsp) whole black pepper
½ oz (15 g/1 tbsp) blades of mace
½ oz (15 g/1 tbsp) whole coriander
1 bay leaf
1 large clove of garlic (optional)

Put the vinegar and spices into a pan. Skin and quarter the clove of garlic if you are using it and add it to the pan. Cover the pan and bring the vinegar very slowly to simmering point. If you leave the vinegar to boil it will evaporate, which is wasteful. Remove the pan from the heat and pour the mixture into a clean basin. Cover and leave the mixture to steep for 6 to 8 hours. After that, strain the vinegar, pour it back into the bottles, screw on the caps tightly and use as required.

It is preferable to use some of the spices suggested rather than all of them each time as this will give your finished pickles the same flavour. Any combination of these spices, including thin slivers of lemon rind and peeled and thinly sliced fresh ginger may be used. Experiment with different mixtures, allowing about 2½ oz (65 g/6 tbsp) mixed whole spices to each 4 pt (2½ l/10 cups) vinegar. Use brown malt vinegar, the cheapest, for dark pickles and chutneys. Distilling brown vinegar gives a white vinegar with a less pungent flavour and this is the kind to use where the finished colour of the vegetables is important, pickled red cabbage for instance.

Uncooked chutney   *makes 5 lb (2¼ kg/5 lb)*

With imperial, metric and American measures it is usually necessary to test each recipe three times, to be sure of satisfactory results whichever measures you decide to use. Joan Cole, a friend who helps me test my recipes, suggested this uncooked recipe, after a day's chutney-making in a steamy kitchen. It's an old farmhouse recipe but otherwise neither of us know its origins.

1 lb (450 g/1 lb) apples
A small piece of fresh root ginger
1 lb (450 g/1 lb) onions
1 lb (450 g/1 lb) stoned dates
1 lb (450 g/1 lb) stoned or seedless raisins
1 lb (450 g/1 lb) dark brown sugar
1 pt (500 ml/2½ cups) malt vinegar
Salt and pepper
Cayenne pepper
1 oz (25 g/3 tbsp) mixed whole pickling spices

Peel, quarter and core the apples and peel the beige skin off the piece of ginger. Skin and quarter the onions. Mince them coarsely with the dates and raisins. Stir in the sugar and vinegar then add 1 tsp (5 ml/1 tsp) salt, a generous amount of freshly ground black or white pepper, and a sprinkle of cayenne pepper. Cayenne pepper is the hot pepper, so be cautious with it unless you like a warm-tasting chutney. Tie the pickling spices in a small piece of muslin and add it to the bowl. Mix thoroughly, then leave the mixture, covered, for 24 hours, stirring it occasionally. Before potting, remove and squeeze out the bag of spices, stir the chutney well and turn it into clean dry jars. Cover, using the jam jar lids which give a good air-tight seal, or failing these, cover the chutney with jam covers, then with pieces of cloth, making an air-tight seal by brushing the cloth thoroughly with melted candle wax. The chutney will keep well in a cool, dark place.

Index